DESIGNING ADULT
SERVICES

DESIGNING ADULT SERVICES

Strategies for Better Serving Your Community

ANN ROBERTS

LIBRARIES
UNLIMITED™

An Imprint of ABC-CLIO, LLC

Santa Barbara, California • Denver, Colorado

Library of Congress Cataloging-in-Publication Data

Names: Roberts, Ann, 1958– author.
Title: Designing adult services : strategies for better serving your community / Ann Roberts.
Description: Santa Barbara, California : Libraries Unlimited, an imprint of ABC-CLIO, LLC, [2018] | Includes bibliographical references and index.
Identifiers: LCCN 2017031516 (print) | LCCN 2017049116 (ebook) | ISBN 9781440852558 (ebook) | ISBN 9781440852541 (paperback : acid-free paper)
Subjects: LCSH: Adult services in public libraries—United States. | Libraries and older people—United States. | Adult services librarians—United States. | Libraries and community—United States.
Classification: LCC Z711.92.A32 (ebook) | LCC Z711.92.A32 R63 2018 (print) | DDC 027.62/20973—dc23
LC record available at https://lccn.loc.gov/2017031516

ISBN: 978–1–4408–5254–1 (paperback)
        978–1–4408–5255–8 (ebook)

22 21 20 19 18   1 2 3 4 5

This book is also available as an eBook.

Libraries Unlimited
An Imprint of ABC-CLIO, LLC

ABC-CLIO, LLC
130 Cremona Drive, P.O. Box 1911
Santa Barbara, California 93116-1911
www.abc-clio.com

This book is printed on acid-free paper ∞

Manufactured in the United States of America

Contents

Acknowledgments

I would like to thank the following individuals, libraries, and library and educational agencies for input and contributions to this work:

Kim Flores, Naphtali Faris, and Michael Anderson, Mid-Continent Public Library, Missouri
Penny Peck, California
Steve Carr, Arlington Public Library, Virginia
Michele Cordero, U. S. Patent and Trademark Office, Virginia
John Paul Myrick, Cross County Library, Arkansas
Linda Hofschire, Colorado State Library, Colorado
John Taube, Allegany County Library, Maryland
Cyndi Lessner, Maryland State Department of Education, Early Childhood Development, Maryland
Jennie Garner, North Liberty Community Library, Iowa
Laurie Orton, San Juan Island Library, Washington
WebJunction, Washington
Urban Libraries Council, District of Columbia

I would also like to thank my dear friend and editor, Blanche Woolls, and my loving husband, Richard Smith, for their encouragement and assistance throughout my library career, and in this and previous publications.

Introduction

ADULT LIBRARY USERS: THEY CAN BE A TOUGH CROWD

If we live long enough, we are adults for much of our lifespan. Childhood and youth go by in a flash, and while they are probably the most important stages in our development and are certainly worthy of all the focus libraries typically give them, they are not the only stages in our development in life. We continue to grow and learn and have different informational needs in all stages of life. According to the Center for Disease Control, the average life expectancy in the United States is 78.8 years (http://www.cdc.gov/nchs/fastats/life-expectancy.htm), and if we consider that in most states in the United States, adulthood begins at age 18, there is a good 60 years in which libraries can and should be serving adults of all ages. And during that 60-year time span, we continue to change and grow almost as much as we did in our youth, if not physically, then certainly intellectually, spiritually, and emotionally. Frequently, changes in life are brought about by life's situations, situations in which we have to learn and adapt to new jobs, new surroundings, new people, new illnesses, having children—the list can go on and on. I have chosen to use a generational approach in this book for following reasons:

1. It makes good sense.
2. It makes the job of serving adults in libraries a little easier, breaking ideas for services and programs down into more manageable increments.
3. It triggers fresh ideas and approaches to providing programs and services.

The stages in life that I have used in this book are loosely based on psychologist Daniel Levinson's theory of adult development (http://study .com/academy/lesson/theories-of-adult-development-levinson-vaillant -neugarten.html). While I understand that many, many people's lives will not fall neatly into the life's experiences and stages outlined either by Dr. Levinson in his research or myself in this book, I have based my ideas of library services to adults on what is often happening in the life stages *of the majority*, beginning with the current youngest generation of adults—the millennials and ending with library services to seniors, the baby boomers. I will address library services to special populations in an additional chapter, but I also count upon the reader to take the suggestions offered in this book and "run with them." Programming ideas for one demographic can easily be tweaked for another. By thinking about what is happening in life's stages, as well as researching local demographics, planning programming and services seems a little less intimidating. Thinking about what each generation has most in common provides a place to begin.

Since the Young Adult Library Services Association (YALSA) of the American Library Association defines young adults as ages 12–18, this book will focus on those "adults" ages 19 and much older. There is a great deal of living and learning to be done after the age of 18, but it is around that time that libraries often lose touch with users who had been faithful attendants of story hour as children and avid fans of library programs as teens. Sometimes it just seems like adults in libraries are a tough crowd.

"But why should that be?" you might wonder.

Because adults are usually very busy people, they have less time for library visits or sometimes even for reading. They are studying, taking classes, working, caring for children, helping out older parents, taking care of homes, planning and nurturing careers and investments and retirement funds, and gasp! There are simply not enough hours in a day for all of these activities.

"So, how can libraries serve this crazy busy portion of the population?" you might ask.

"By making their lives better, and maybe even just a little easier," would be the correct response.

"And why the generational approach?" you might be wondering. If you have lived long enough, you will easily recognize that as we age, we become very different people along the way. I can assure you, I am nothing like I was in my 20s, much to the relief of many people who were genuinely concerned about my well-being. And it does happen almost by decade. Things just change. Our bodies change, our minds change, our life's circumstances change, and we have different information needs.

Libraries can serve adults of all ages in many ways, by offering convenience in access to good information, technology, lifelong learning, and an intellectually stimulating outing for children, their parents, and grandparents. There is something to be found for every age group at the library. I have, by no means, come up with an exhaustive list of programs and services for each age group but rather hope to inspire the library community to take a generational approach to library service when planning for programs and services. Tailoring library programs to varying age groups not only better serves the public but also makes the job of the librarian easier, once we recognize those varying information needs at various stages in life. Programs and suggested ideas for collection development in each chapter can obviously be used for other age groups, but I offer them as suggestions for specific age groups, according to life's stages. Each chapter in the book will offer simple programming ideas, with more detailed programs described at the end of Chapters 2–9, or those chapters devoted to serving specific demographics.

Libraries can offer a sanctuary for a quiet breather, a place to connect with communities or be directed to the right place to find the help we need at various stressful junctures in life. Libraries can provide all of this and so much more, if we put our minds and our hearts into it. So, go out and give those busy, diverse, information seeking adults the break the need today!

CHAPTER 1

Planning for Library Services to Adults

As with any library service, library services to adults require planning and monitoring for successes and failures. Determining the type of programming and services that your particular community responds well to and knowing the demographics of your local population are important components of successful library service. In one smaller city library in a relatively rural area where I planned programs for adults, I was surprised to find that the seniors in the region really loved poetry and would attend poetry programs, particularly those in which they could share their own original poetry. It was the senior version of the poetry slam before poetry slams were "a thing"! Music and original musical compositions were also very popular in this region. Figuring out what works and what does not work in your local community is as much a part of the job as learning library collections and getting a feel for how to work with coworkers and volunteers in the workplace.

KNOW THY COMMUNITY

Looking at local demographics can go a long way toward helping you with planning for adult services. If your community is heavily populated with seniors, you know that you should devote more resources to programming and services to older adults. If your community is largely made up of young professionals, you can easily focus programs and services on this demographic. This type of assessment will assist you in marketing toward specific demographics, as different marketing techniques often will reach different user groups.

Using U.S. Census Bureau tools like American FactFinder and American Community Survey will glean general demographic information, such as population age and number of households by number of occupants. This type of information can be obtained by zip code, which offers a clearer picture of inhabitants in the library's vicinity.

Another way to segment the adult population in your service area is by using ESRI Tapestry (http://www.esri.com/data/tapestry). This product allows you to search by zip code and see the demographics of the residents of a specific zip code area. This product is also helpful in determining the number of people of any particular demographic segment in your service area. While this is a product from a vendor, as opposed to free statistics from the Census Bureau, it might be worth the investment.

Another great resource is your own library statistics. Take a look at those statistics. What are the most popular services you offer in the form of web-based services? What is "hot" in library circulation? What could you improve? Your library's circulation system can provide a snapshot of library users, depending upon the types of statistics your library gathers and stores, and you may find information on the usage of various age groups, zip code service areas, and so on. Reports drawing on circulation data may reveal trends as well as the types of materials that circulate most. Taking a look at reports generated by the Integrated Library System (ILS) can give you a better idea of what is and is not currently circulating and information about library users, helping you determine where to put more of your precious and limited resources. Upticks in specific subject area searches and checkouts can also provide inspiration for new programming ideas.

Also consider the other agencies within your library's service area, such as senior centers, arts organizations, and social services agencies, as potential partners, as sources of information, and as indicators of the demographics of people living in your area. Are there a number of senior centers and other service organizations for seniors in the area? Are there more hot spots for younger adults? Is there a community arts center? All of these agencies can serve as resources and partners for library projects and programs. This type of information can lead to expanding library services or provide another outlet for marketing current library services as well as indicators of demographics and potential need for library services to these demographics. If there is a local agency serving immigrant populations, for example, the library should definitely have a presence there, whether in the form of outreach and visits or through welcoming flyers available to the agency. If there are senior centers in the area, you should consider doing some outreach there, if you have not already done so. Learning about local agencies and working with them can be a boon to the library in the form of generating new users and new community supporters.

SURVEY THYSELF: CUSTOMER SATISFACTION
AND EVALUATING SERVICES

Surveying library users should really be an ongoing endeavor. Every time you offer a program, gauge the success with a follow-up evaluation. Ask for recommendations for future programs. Debrief with presenters after a program to gauge their feeling for audience interest and participation. Have an online library survey, which library users can access any time or do an annual customer satisfaction survey, marketing the link to the online survey in newsletters and other publications. Many libraries and museums provide preloaded iPads to gather feedback as customers are leaving their venue or program. For time-strapped tech-savvy users, this method can provide a higher completion rate than sending paper home with customers. For the technologically challenged, if nothing else, provide paper copies and a place to deposit them. Listen to complaints; listen to suggestions. Have physical and digital suggestion boxes, prominently displayed, and actually check them from time to time.

Community or "town hall"–style meetings are a great way to really get to know what the local citizenry would like from the library. There are always people who will show up and tell you what is on their minds. More revealing too can be the absence of a certain demographic. If you find that younger people do not show up to a program or event at the library, host a similar event in a favorite hot spot out in the community. Mingle among the people and eventually you will get to know your community and your users, and you'll be inspired to come up with new ways to reach new users.

When evaluating library programs, be sure to ask questions about what the participants found useful or meaningful in the program and what they would like to see in future programs. Follow up with library staff about the success or failure of programs, too. Evaluations allow us to determine how well a program is working and have the evidence in hand to support its continuation or the evidence to implement change. Evaluations are much easier to create from the desired outcomes for every program, by ensuring the outcomes match with what the program is intended to present. Additionally, attendance records, connectivity to other programs and library materials' potential, and patron feedback should be included with all evaluations.

For convenience, sample general library surveys of varying lengths, courtesy of Library Research Service of the Colorado State Library, can be found in Appendix A.

Goals with Gusto

When planning for library services to adults, create goals that are broad enough to define the overall picture of intent, including goals for professional accomplishment. Make sure that goals are clear and concise yet broad enough to allow for accomplishing them. Can they be updated from year to year by way of "raising the bar"? Are they flexible enough to meet changes in technology and trends and changing community and library-wide values?

An example of a comprehensive goal for adult services would be "Enhance local knowledge of e-government resources," through a year-long series of programs, emphasis emphasizing resources, and staff awareness. Some action-based objectives in accomplishing this goal would be as follows:

- Assemble a team to focus on web resources and sharing information with other staff through presentations and compilations of resources.
- Work with tech personnel to create an e-government resources page with links to various e-government resources on the library website.
- Provide a monthly program, blog posts, or newsletter articles highlighting different areas of e-government.
- Promote e-government resources via library marketing outlets.
- Create a list of easily measurable outcomes for the goal that will later serve as evaluative measures, such as the following:

  1. _____ (number of) people will attend a program on e-government resources in the next year.
  2. Word of mouth and marketing will create an increase in the number of program participants as the year progresses.
  3. Hits on the e-government resources page will increase over the course of the year.
  4. At least one of the programs will receive media attention.
  5. At least two of the programs will receive requests for more information about a given topic.

Evaluating the Success of Specific Programs

Specific programs need to have customized evaluations, based upon already established goals and expected outcomes and using quantitative as well as qualitative measures. So, for example, if you are having a program on changing careers in mid-life, the goal for the program might be,

"Attendees will find out more about successfully changing careers in mid-life." The expected outcomes for this program might be as follows:

1. Circulation of books on career change will be up.
2. Attendees will seek assistance with online career resources referenced in the presentation.
3. The majority of attendees will report that they learned something useful from the presentation.
4. The majority of attendees will report a positive reaction to the program.
5. The guest speaker will report positive feedback about the experience.
6. Patron attendance will be higher than previous programs through marketing and word of mouth.

Evaluative Survey Questions

Evaluative questions for your survey can be devised from your expected outcomes. For example:

1. After attending this program, do you anticipate seeking out library materials on the subject of career changes in midlife?
2. After attending this program, will you use online career resources suggested in the presentation?
3. Did you learn something useful about career changes in midlife during this program?
4. What was your favorite part of the program and will you attend similar programs in the future?
5. Will you tell friends about this program or invite friends to future, similar library programs?

By having clearly stated outcomes for programs, it is easy enough to create informative and evaluative follow-up surveys to determine the success, or failure, of a program.

Evaluating Technology Services

The Edge Initiative is a suite of tools that assists libraries in planning for technology services and identifying areas that need improvement. The Edge Toolkit provides libraries an overview of current public services and community engagement as they relate to the public's use of technology in the library. Led by the Urban Libraries Council, the Edge Initiative was funded by the Bill and Melinda Gates Foundation.

With 11 benchmarks, the Edge Initiative launched nationally in 2014. Edge allows libraries to assess the use of public access technology, identify specific ways to strengthen or enhance public access technologies, and determine ways to engage community leaders about the library's role in serving the technology needs of local communities. These benchmarks address the types and depth of technology training libraries offer, staff technology competencies, needs assessment, and engagement of community leaders in planning for technology usage and growth.

Benchmark 4.2, "The library gathers feedback from the community about its public technology needs," suggests that libraries should gather feedback from the community about technology needs through the following:

- An analysis of the social and economic conditions of the community is conducted as part of information gathering for strategic planning and decision making.
- Questions about community technology are included in a library-sponsored needs assessment survey.
- Community technology–related questions are included in a local government survey.
- The library holds advertised forums on the community's technology needs.
- The library conducts a community needs assessment for technology resources in languages other than English.
- The library conducts a community needs assessment for technology resources for people with disabilities.

Understanding community technology needs, while possibly exposing some inadequacies in library technology services, can only serve to improve services in the future and make planning and working with local government officials easier.

To learn more about the Edge Initiative and a variety of benchmarks that will assist you in serving diverse library communities, visit http://www.libraryedge.org/about-edge.

KNOW THYSELF AND THY STAFF: COMPETENCIES IN SERVING ADULTS

Just like librarians who serve children and young adults need special competencies or knowledge, so does the librarian who serves adults. As a former adult services consultant for a state library, I worked with the implementation of WebJunction in Missouri, an online resource for librarians. WebJunction lists 12 competencies for adult services librarians in the "Competency Index for the Library Field 2014." This document is a compilation of a number of competencies defined by other library organizations, including the American Library Association, numerous state technology competencies, and the Special Library Association's Competencies for Information Professionals in the 21st Century. This listing of competencies encompasses library services to adults and older adults as well as children, young adults, and so on. These 12 competencies for adult services librarians, promoting good library service to adults in the areas of outreach, programming, readers' advisory, and reference, are as follows:

- Design and implement library services to engage and meet the needs of the community
- Design and implement outreach services for the library community to increase use of library services and to reach underserved populations
- Use online tools and communities to engage with and provide services to users
- Design, implement, and sponsor library programs that provide opportunities for information, entertainment, and lifelong learning
- Design and implement library services to meet the needs and interests of older adults in the community
- Develop a wide variety of services to meet the needs and interests of older adults and of their families and caregivers, as members of the Sandwich Generation
- Design, implement, and sponsor library programs for older adults that provide information, entertainment, and opportunities for lifelong learning
- Assist users with choosing popular and recreational reading, viewing, and listening choices
- Develop strategies and sources to stay well informed as a readers' advisor
- Demonstrate ability to meet information-seeking needs of users
- Develop and maintain a collection of reference resources to meet community needs
- Facilitate library users' requests for information

This compilation of competencies is a good starting point for determining if you or your staff need to "bone up" in the knowledge and skills needed to serve library users in any of these demographics and offer additional guidance as to the types of services and programs you should be offering your adult library users. The complete competencies for library services to adults, including further criteria for achieving each of the competencies listed here, can be found in Appendix B. The entire publication for all areas of library service can be found at WebJunction.org (https://www.webjunction.org/documents/webjunction/Competency_Index_for_the_Library_Field.html).

IMPROVE THYSELF: PROFESSIONAL DEVELOPMENT FOR ADULT SERVICES LIBRARIANS

Many states offer or require public library certification, which involves taking a number of online or on-site continuing education (CE) courses for credit and maintaining CE credits after certification, and consequently offer tremendous CE opportunities to support this requirement. Other states simply offer continuing education for the sake of professional development and improving library skills in an ever-changing work environment. Some state libraries also offer certificates of completion to residents outside the home state, when completing online courses. The Idaho Commission for Libraries, which requires library certification for those without library science degrees, has two complete online courses, Alternative Basic Library Education (ABLE) and Supplemental Alternative Basic Library Education (SABLE), and offers certificates of completion for distance users (http://libraries.idaho.gov/Continuing Education). These courses can be particularly useful for paraprofessional staff, as the basis for library service that they did not attain by completing a library science degree.

Having worked in continuing education for library workers, I was constantly looking for professional development outlets and collaborating with public library staff to create new CE opportunities. We provided webinars, single or half-day seminars, and an annual multiday training event for library workers around the state of Missouri, all geared toward working with adults in libraries. One of the most convenient tools that I worked with was WebJunction.

WebJunction is a great resource for professional development and continuing education. WebJunction offers library-specific courses and webinar archives free to all library workers and volunteers, made possible by the support of OCLC, the Gates Foundation, and the Institute of Museum and Library Services. WebJunction offers self-paced courses in a number of subject areas that would benefit the adult services librarian, including collection development, public services, technical services, customer service, programming and advocacy, and outreach. The archived webinars feature librarians from all walks, independent trainers, and consultants in presentations in any number of subjects. Archived webinars can be accessed at any time, and free monthly webinars are compiled by the Wyoming State Library and posted on WebJunction each month. The free webinar listing can be found at http://www.webjunction.org/find-training/free-events.html. These archived webinars provide a rich resource for brief refreshers on any number of subjects. You can also sign up for full self-paced WebJunction courses at http://learn.webjunction.org/.

If the free professional development opportunities are not "making the grade" for you, there are any number of fee-based services out there, such as Library Juice Academy, Infopeople, and Click University. The important thing is to continue to grow and improve in ways that benefit your library users.

CONCLUSION

Knowing your community, knowing your staff, understanding your users' technology needs, and knowing your own strengths and weaknesses make for a better opportunity to grow and expand, both as library professionals and with your library services and programs. Do a little investigation into your local demographics, set aside some time for professional growth for yourself and your staff each month, and see what happens!

CHAPTER 2

Waiting in the Wings: Age Group 19–24

When we think of library services to adults, a fairly large swath of the population falls into that category and encompasses a wide demographic. We are talking about a whole bunch of people here, all with varying interests and information needs at various stages in their lives. When taking the broad view of library services to adults, creating good programs and helpful services might seem like a daunting challenge, but as with most library services, taking small steps to improve on current service or incrementally implementing new services can be a means to success.

Although libraries have been serving adults for centuries, it was not until the mid-twentieth century when the American Library Association (ALA) created the Adult Services Division of ALA. At this time, the organization decided to create a separate division, recognizing that adults in libraries might have different information needs than children and teens, and therefore guidelines for library services to adults were established in order to provide better service for them. And library services to adults not only encompass a wide demographic but a wide range of services as well: Programming, reference, circulation services, services to special populations, and outreach can all fall into this very broad category.

In this chapter, we will focus on those emerging adults who are "waiting in the wings"—the 19–24-year-olds who are planning on or are working toward careers or hoping to move up in their chosen field, as they gain experience in the classroom or the workplace.

MILLENNIALS: "ADULTOLESCENTS" OR EMERGING ADULTS?

In June 2015, the U.S. Census Bureau issued a press release proclaiming that Millennials had become the largest demographic in the United

States. The millennial wave of people born between 1982 and 2000 marks an increase in ethnic diversity, as pointed out in the Census Bureau's news release, with 44.2 percent of millennials being of a minority race or ethnic group (http://www.census.gov/newsroom/ press-releases/2015/cb15-113.html). Millennials, like other generations, have a number of common characteristics. They are more politically liberal, less likely to be religious, and do not have the kind of work/life delineations of previous generations, which in some respects is a good thing, and in others, not so much. Millennials are also more likely to still be living at home after the economic downturn of 2008 than the same demographic during the Great Depression, even though the job market and economy have made a recovery, for the time being (http://www.pewsocialtrends.org/2015/07/29/more-millennials-living -with-family-despite-improved-job-market/).

In "The Millennial Generation, 'Keep Calm and Carry On,' " Neil Howe notes that during the millennials' childhood years, late baby boomers and early Generation Xers, now having families of their own, brought "family" to the forefront, raising awareness of child abuse and child safety issues, and manufactured child-friendly and safer minivans to haul their little ones from one after-school event to another. Politicians and Madison Avenue began defining all sorts of adult issues in terms of their effects on their children, and marketing directly to kids became the norm. "But what about the children?"—some audience members were bound to ask on daytime TV talk shows, no matter the subject of the day! Howe suggests that "given all this adult attention, it's no wonder that this rising generation has developed a sense of specialness, to themselves, to their parents, and to the wider community" (http://www.forbes.com/sites/ neilhowe/2014/09/04/the-millennial-generation-keep-calm-and-carry-on -part-6-of-7/).

So, given the amount of attention that they saw growing up, millennials have tremendous expectations for their careers, their ideas, and how things should work. Baby boomers and millennials do not always see eye to eye, but with millennials now outnumbering baby boomers, their attitudes toward everything-technology, work, consumerism, marriage and sex, and so on will obviously influence the way we work, play, study, and live. They already do. A more relaxed attitude can be found in workplaces from the t-shirt- and jeans-clad hipsters of Silicon Valley to the everyday practice of checking e-mail and social media before getting down to work now commonplace in so many professional settings (http://communitytable.parade.com/274485/paultaylor/boomers-and -millennials-bridging-the-generation-gap/).

Although they are the generation that has stayed at home the longest, millennials are willing to be mobile for career-related reasons and consequently find themselves in new communities looking for the type of assistance a library can provide. According to "Reason for Moving: 2012 to 2013," published by the U.S. Census Bureau, the 25–29-year-old demographic is the group most often moving for career and work, landing a good job, and setting the stage for the next phase in life, focused more on family and achievement (https://www.census.gov/prod/2014pubs/p20-574.pdf).

Adultolescenthood

The first instance of the term "adultolescent" that I could locate in my research was in an article published in 2002 in *Newsweek* magazine, titled "Bringing up Adultolescents" by Peg Tyre (http://www.newsweek.com/bringing-adultolescents-141705). It is an interesting term and one that caught my eye while reading another article about millennials. So, while the rise in the number of twentysomethings still living at home increased after the economic downturn of 2008, it seems that the issue has been recognized prior to that time. Jeffrey Arnett, a psychology professor at Clark University in Worcester, Massachusetts, proposes that people in their 20s (the chronological age of most millennials right now) are at a separate stage in life's development, a stage he calls the "emerging adult"—young people who are not yet ready to take on the responsibilities normally relegated to the adult. He also proposes that this transition from dependent child at home *to adult is currently happening at a slower pace*. His theory is that the cultural and economic changes that have led to a need for more education in our information-based society, as well as fewer entry-level jobs, and a greater societal acceptance of premarital sex and cohabitation has created a greater state of "limbo" for young people in the late twentieth and the twenty-first centuries.

According to a recent article in the *Washington Post*, younger millennials—those born in the 1990s—are more than twice as likely to be sexually *inactive* in their early twenties as older millennials or even the previous generation (https://www.washingtonpost.com/local/social-issues/there-isnt-really-anything-magical-about-it-why-more-millennials-are-putting-off-sex/2016/08/02/e7b73d6e-37f4-11e6-8f7c-d4c723a2becb_story.html). The article cites issues over sexual consent, career ambitions, lack of personal contact, and the use of online dating services, which focus on physical appearance as well as the prevalence of online pornography as contributing factors to the blasé attitudes toward mating found in these younger millennials. So, with younger men and women focusing more on career and education and less on starting families, we have a demographic of younger people delaying entry into what was traditionally the adult world of marriage and family (http://www.nytimes.com/2010/08/22/magazine/22Adulthood-t.html?pagewanted=all&_r=0).

If emerging adults or millennials have specific psychological and emotional needs at this point in their development, it must follow that they have different information needs as well, generally relating to career preparation and higher education. Public libraries, by tweaking their current collections, including electronic resources, and offering specific programs, can keep some of those once-enthusiastic members of the teen advisory board as library supporters for years to come.

Attitudes toward Libraries

According to Kathryn Zickuhr, Lee Rainie, and Kristen Purcell, in an article posted by the Pew Internet and American Life Project, younger Americans ages 16–29 serve up a mixed bag of habits and preferences when it comes to reading, libraries, and technology. While almost all younger people are online and make use of online resources, they are also more likely than older patrons to use the libraries' computer and Internet connections. They are also likely to say that they have read at least one book in print in the past year (2012), more so than adults ages 30 and older, perhaps the result of being enrolled in college or trade school. Younger Americans are just as likely as older adults to visit the library, borrow print materials, and browse the shelves, and the majority of younger adults say it is "very important" for libraries to have librarians for assistance in the library and materials for check out. Few think that libraries should automate library services or do away with printed materials.

That being said, younger people are still more likely to use the library's computers or the library's online research resources, such as online databases. Sixty percent of younger patrons say they go to the library to study, sit, and read, or watch or listen to media as compared to 45 percent of older patrons, and everyone agrees that libraries should provide more comfortable spaces for reading, working, and relaxing (http://libraries.pewinternet.org/2013/06/25/younger-americans-library-services/).

LIBRARY SERVICES FOR THE EMERGING ADULT

In many areas, libraries are partnered with state employment agencies, sometimes in the same building or nearby. This kind of partnership provides "one stop shopping" for job seekers, finding assistance with resume preparation, practice tests, and the opportunity to register for or search with state employment agencies. In the state of Missouri, where I served as adult services consultant for the Missouri State Library, we partnered with the Division of Workforce Development to educate library workers about the types of services provided by one-stop career centers. In many instances, local libraries were already working with career centers, particularly in rural areas. Developing job skills and career-development remain at the top of the list for many millennials and point to the need for job skills and career services in libraries.

The Hartford, Connecticut, Public Library, in partnership with CTWorks, lists the following workforce development services on its website:

Core services:

- Internet access
- Job leads
- Online job application assistance
- Resume creation and revision
- Professional resume critique
- Career counseling
- Information on job fairs and recruitments
- Career services information session
- Impact interviewing workshop
- Online job training and testing with Metrix Learning Online
- Career planning with Career Edge
- Interactive courses, video-based simulations, and assessments
- Test preparation resources
- Company information resources
- Books, DVDs, and online resources about job searching, resumes, careers, and interviewing
- Links to helpful websites
- Lists of local temp agencies
- Referrals to job training, education, community agencies, and intensive services

Special services:

- Ex-Offender Employment and Retention Program

Related services also at the library:

- Computer classes
- English language classes
- Immigration and citizenship assistance
- General Equivalency Diploma (GED) preparation resources
- Online High School Diploma program
- Math tutoring and materials

For more information about this collaboration between the Hartford Public Library and CTWorks, visit http://www.hplct.org/library-services/job-career.

In most cases, online databases are also available to library card holders outside the library. These databases offer everything from GED preparation, resume building, and interview preparation skills. Partnering with local career centers and promoting online tools are a couple of the many ways libraries can help prepare those emerging adults who are waiting in the wings to take their place in the spotlight.

A Second Chance

How about this wonderful collaboration? Chattanooga (Tennessee) Public Library (CPL), in partnership with Gale/Cengage Learning, offered library patrons the opportunity to earn an accredited high school diploma and credentialed career certificate online. This collaboration with Career Online High School (COHS) served as a unique pilot program allowing adult learners to finish high school online while also receiving additional career training.

CPL awarded full scholarships to qualified adult learners who completed an online self-assessment, prerequisite course, and on-site interview. The scholarship provided enrolled students with an academic coach as well as access to board certified instructors to provide support throughout the course. While this type of collaboration could benefit adults beyond the age range of emerging adult, it is often this demographic that looks back at missed opportunities to obtain a high school diploma when trying to enter the job market. Some students were able to complete the course in as little as four to six months by transferring previously earned high school credits. These students were provided 24/7 access to the online learning platform, which makes it easier to get a degree if work or family schedules are conflicting. A high school diploma can only improve the chances of landing a better job, and a collaboration such as this puts the local library in the unique position to fulfill a mission of lifelong learning to a demographic in need (http://chattlibrary.org/content/library-resources-spotlight-librarys-ged-prep-options). To learn more about Gale/Cengage COHS, visit http://www.careeronlinehs.gale.com.

Joint-Use Libraries

While the bulk of library usage for most college students will happen in the academic library, public libraries can also continue to play an important role in the academic life of the average college student or student in career training. In fact, public and academic libraries have "joined forces" in many areas, creating joint-use libraries. The San Jose Public Library in California, which is a collaboration between the San Jose Public Library and San Jose State University, is such an example. According to the Mission Statement published in the original agreement, December 17, 1998, "The purpose of the Joint Library is to provide both the University community and the residents of the City with a high quality library dedicated to providing excellent service to all of its users and providing access to an extensive collection of library materials" (http://www.sjlibrary.org/files_king/documents/operating_agreement.pdf).

There are many other examples of joint-use libraries, including partnerships with community college libraries and even public school libraries in rural areas. Sometimes the local school library is the only library in a rural area, and school libraries can provide a great service to the general public. In urban areas, joint use libraries, such as the San Jose Public Library, joint-use libraries can provide access to materials not always found in a public library, benefiting both the general public and the student body as well as general reading material, programming, and access to online resources. By pooling resources, a higher standard of service and library collections can be achieved in some cases.

In my own experience as a reference librarian in a town with two universities nearby, I constantly helped students who came to the public library for assistance, as the academic libraries were either short-staffed or simply not as pleasant or the staff as helpful as the staff in our little public library. Frequently, students of higher education can have access to online databases and other materials in general areas of study at a public library, comparable to that which they would find in the academic library. While public libraries cannot provide all of the collections an academic library might, the public library can offer a supportive and helpful environment in which college students and those in career training can seek assistance or make use of online databases, which might just be the edge that some students need.

An Enhanced Library Catalog, Digital Services, Blogs, and Tweets

I remember back when dinosaurs roamed the earth, my husband very proudly showed me how he "Telnetted" to a library catalog and located a book for me.

"See? There it is!" he crowed, sitting at a computer monitor, which resembled the head of a giant alien, resting on our kitchen table.

"So what's it about?" I asked, causing his face to fall to his chest. My information need was much greater than he had anticipated.

Having a library catalog with book reviews, including the capacity to allow patrons to review books, is a great way to appeal to younger people. Born at a time when social networking online was becoming "the thing," younger adults are accustomed to being able to contribute to discussions, and finding a book review in the library catalog prevents them from having to look one up in another place. Allowing patrons to provide their own book reviews incorporates an element of social networking into something that every library has online. Book reviews, right where you want them, is a good thing for any age group!

Library blogs are also a great way to get information out to patrons, even allowing them to comment and share in blog posts. Blogs can provide useful information about library services, books, or upcoming programs, above and beyond the standard description of what can be found in a particular database or a calendar of events. Blogs can also be a way to continue the educational experience provided by a program or presentation, offer book and film reviews, and so much more.

Tumblr and Twitter

Many libraries use Tumblr and Twitter for keeping in touch with library users. Tumblr can best be described as a social networking site and a blog, frequently described as a "microblog" as one is more likely to find images and short snippets of information on Tumblr, as opposed to the more traditional, journal-style blogging. Tumblr has over 217 million separate blogs with 420 million users and has been in use since 2007.

Tumblr allows a person to create a web page that is a collection of things they like and want to share, such as images, music clips, and text, and also reblog from other Tumblr feeds. This is very appealing for younger adults trying to connect with other people with similar interests.

Twitter is a free social networking microblog service that allows registered members to broadcast posts of 140 characters or less, referred to as "tweets." Twitter members can tweet themselves and follow other users' tweets on multiple platforms and devices. The act of adding a meta tag, referred to as a hashtag, written as #keyword, can create conversation threads or connect users to a general topic such as #yourlibrary. Tweets are permanent and are searchable on the Twitter website. Tweeting brief reminders about upcoming events, new books, or other library acquisitions, or simple reminders about library closings, and so on would be a simple way to use Twitter.

Digital Services

Digital services, which every generation will use but are a must for younger library users, include online access to the following:

- Digital magazines (Zinio)
- Downloadable audiobooks
- e-Books
- Movies (IndieFlix, Overdrive)
- Music (Freegal)
- Hoopla

Access to digital services such as hoopla provides free movies, television series, music, audio, and e-books to library users through their library card. Just be sure that while users are browsing through online offerings, they also see notice of some interesting in-house or partnership programs or classes that also suit their needs and interests.

COLLECTION DEVELOPMENT AND PROGRAMS

Reading: Genre Fiction

While young millennials might get more of their *information* from on-line sources, apparently they are still fans of reading old-fashioned print books. Having a library that includes an ample collection of reading materials for this age group, as well as interesting programming, is key to drawing them in. At a time when reading textbooks and manuals takes up a great deal of time, a little reading for pleasure can restore a sense of adventure, play, peace, or simple escapism for the budding adult reader.

The burgeoning world of genre fiction offers up many new choices for readers today. Genres that at one time only appealed to a small niche of readers have exploded into big markets with big followings. Some of these newer genres that appeal to younger adults include the following:

- Steampunk: A subgenre of science fiction set in Victorian times or a futuristic time when steam is once again the main source of machine power.
- Urban fiction: Used for works set in urban America often dealing with drugs, violence, and sex, involving African American or Latino characters. The genre is also known as Street Fiction, Gangsta Lit, Ghetto Lit, or Hip-Hop Fiction.
- Chick lit: Addresses issues of modern womanhood, generally not considered a subcategory of the romance genre, as the subject matter focuses on relationships and issues not necessarily related to romantic life.
- Graphic novels: Stories, usually science fiction or fantasy, told mainly through illustrations in comic strip format; not so much a genre as a format.
- Paranormal romance: Romance stories between paranormal entities such as vampires, ghosts, elves, fairies, and so on.
- Queer fiction: Focuses on issues of the LGBT community, including romance, sexual relationships, prejudice, family relationships, and so on.
- NA (New adult): Featuring protagonists in their late teens and early 20s, with more sexually explicit content than young adult fiction— think *Losing It* by Cora Carmack.

There are a number of online tools that can assist in identifying books in specific genres, such as Goodreads; the Reading List, published annually by the Collection Development and Evaluation section of the Reference and User Services Association of ALA, which highlights outstanding genre fiction and includes read-alikes (http://www.ala.org/rusa/sections/codes); Genrefluent (www.genrefluent.com); and subscription services like NoveList, by EBSCO. Online genre browsing or searching, as well as searching by the "appeal" or feel of the book, are both terrific ways to identify books that appeal to a particular age group. ALA's

Booklist and Booklist online are subscription services offering book reviews for all genres. Book awards lists are also great tools for finding books in a specific genre, such as the Edgar Award for mysteries, the Street Literature award for urban fiction, and the Hugo and Galileo awards for science fiction.

Acing the Test

Testing seems to come up pretty often for this demographic, whether it is for a college course, identifying career aptitude, obtaining a license or certificate, or job readiness. Test preparation is big, and whether it is done online with practice tests or through study of a printed source, making sure that twentysomethings are aware of the resources available at the library is vital. Texts for test preparation are still a high-circulation item, and the choices in test preparation textbooks are many. Examples of test preparation texts for emerging adults would include the following:

- ASVAB (Armed Services Vocational Aptitude Battery): Preparation for military testing
- Civil Service exams: Postal service, government clerical, accounting, and so on
- Praxis: National teacher examinations
- GED preparation
- GRE, LSAT, SAT, MAT: Graduate school entrance exams

Acing the Test Electronically

Electronic resources are at everyone's fingertips all the time, and far too many people think that if they found it online, it must be a good source. It is up to librarians and other educators to dispel this myth and offer credible resources to our users. Emerging adults, engaged in study and preparation for work and career, need access to reliable, credible electronic resources and libraries, more than any other institution, serve this up every day. While students can Google to their heart's content, who knows if what they are finding is accurate and reliable information? Studying and practicing for a test using reliable and up-to-date sources provided by a trusted institution like the local public library is a service that any emerging adult can and should use. By providing remote access to electronic resources to anyone with a library card and an electronic device, libraries make the study life of their users so much easier.

Access to these resources can vary widely, based upon an institution's budget, but here are a few to be aware of:

- Learning Express Library: Includes prep and testing for many occupations, such as health, civil service, cosmetology, emergency medical services, firefighting, law enforcement, nursing, teaching, and grad school preparation.
- Gale Courses: Instructor-led courses available online in the areas of accounting, business, health care, language, law, writing, and publishing.
- Occupational Outlook online: U.S. Department of Labor's guide to careers, describing the training and education needed, job prospects, job descriptions, working conditions, and average salary.
- Safari Books online: Resume writing and building, interview techniques.

Programming Ideas: Millennial Approved

Twentysomethings still need a place to hang out with friends, and if they do not want the local bar scene, a coffee shop is usually the answer. On Reddit.com, a social media and social news aggregate website, self-described as "the front page of the Internet," I found a wish list of sorts for libraries, posted by people in their 20s:

- Providing a space for a coffee shop and then having an outside company (a small, local business, or a chain) set up shop in the space
- Being open Friday/Saturday nights for those who do not necessarily want to go out partying every weekend
- Have comfortable reading spots with good lighting, perhaps facing a window or fireplace (maybe a fake one) in the winter
- Used book sales
- Talks/concerts/events: Anything from classical music to local author talks, to local farmers or gardeners giving a talk/demonstration on backyard gardening
- A meeting place
- Art exhibits
- Anything with free food
- Having a liquor license (and good insurance) for special events
- Being able to check out more expensive board games like Settlers of Catan, Ticket To Ride, Cards against Humanity, Dungeons and

Dragons, Exploding Kittens and Mystery Express, and board game tournaments for these types of games
* Discussion groups for current events and books or books versus "the movie"

The Big Brother, Big Sister Influence

Younger children look up to their older siblings, aunts and uncles, sports figures, and celebrities, and we all play a role in how we influence the young. The old adage "It takes a village to raise a child" is most evident in library culture and practices. New adults are in the perfect position to instill the love of libraries and lifelong learning into youngsters over which they have influence. Recent high school graduates, looking for college or career opportunities, can help educate middle school and high school–age kids about the process of applying for college and choosing the right school. Learning about these steps in life from an older relative or cool older friend might have more impact than the local school counselor.

In addition to providing multigenerational programming for parents, grandparents, and children, consider taking it a step further, with Big Brother, Big Sister programming. While kids expect to get special attention from parents and grandparents, a big brother, sister, or friend offering to read with a child or take a child to a program at the library could have great results. An example program follows in the More Detailed Programming Ideas section of this chapter.

At this stage in the game of life, as in most other stages, people need something to draw them into the library and, most importantly, to be made aware of events and services the library is offering (https://www .reddit.com/r/Libraries/comments/2go4v3/what_brings_20_and_30_year _old_patrons_to_the/).

MORE DETAILED PROGRAMMING IDEAS

Program: Big Board Games at the Library

In the past decade, the popularity of board games has grown exponentially, going far beyond the board games of my youth, such as Monopoly and Life. These board games vary in complexity, style, mechanics, visual interest, and a host of other ways. In addition to the popularity of online gaming, actual board games are making a big comeback.

Learning goals:

- Enjoy more expensive and challenging board games with like-minded individuals
- Learn new skills from games
- Learn about additional library resources, such as books, e-books, online videos, and movie collections related to the games

Steps to take:
(Using these tips from WebJunction, "Board in the Library, Part One, An Introduction to Designer Board Games," by John Pappas, December 30, 2013, http://www.webjunction.org/news/webjunction/board-in-the-library-part-six.html)

- Keep game nights relatively small; four participants per three games seem ideal.
- Promote and communicate on library blog, Meetup, and the library's Facebook page. Ask interested parties to share freely.
- Teach one game per event, but do not take on the role of player.
- Allow those familiar with games already to take a leading role as well.
- Try to learn about skill level and interest in certain games beforehand.
- Prepare to host additional nights if interest level exceeds the maximum recommended number of participants.
- Consider having separate nights for more difficult games and simpler games so that gamers may "graduate" in skill levels.
- Have three games of varying themes, rules, and mechanics, on separate tables in a room away from the public areas.
- Have enough seating for all players.
- Consider inviting "watchers" who want to learn, without being intrusive.
- Try to have additional moderators, if you do not feel up to moderating three games at once.

There are so many new board games from which to choose. Popular Mechanics (PM) offers a quick look at the best new games of 2017. I am sure if you ask local gamers, you will find out which might work best for your local community. Here are some of the best new games from PM online:

Grand Austria Hotel allows up to four players to take charge of turn-of-the-century Viennese cafes and hotels, using management and staff skills such as marketing to customers, filling their food and drink orders, and assigning rooms. Points are made by balancing six goals at once, and at the beginning of each round, a random toss of dice affects players' options.

Quadropolis might be a game for the less outgoing players. With few player interactions, it can feel a bit like solitaire; but every library has its share of introverts! In Quadropolis, up to four players build a custom metropolis from scratch, by sending out a team of four architects, gathering plans for various buildings in four rounds, and then constructing them in a four-by-four city map grid. Points are awarded by how and where buildings are constructed.

Scythe is a steampunk-themed reimagining of 1920s Europe, which calls for five players at a hexagonal game board. While it is not a combat-centric game, Scythe might require players to complete a quest to steal food and money from the locals, build a mine to connect territories, and plan a raid into a Soviet territory to do battle with coal-powered machinery in order to steal their iron.

Coffee House Concert Series

A "grown up," casual vibe would be good for the Coffee House Concert Series. Most towns, no matter how large or small, have some local musicians or musicians somewhere within a 50 mile radius who would be interested in sharing their talent. A series of free musical events, set up with table and chairs "coffee house style," might be fun for those who do not want to party all the time. Offer a variety of musicians, reflecting different musical styles, and allow for Q&A.

Learning goals:

- Learn about different musical genres
- Learn about library music resources
- Learn about local musicians

Steps to take:

- Have a budget-using local talent, which should not mean "free" talent, and at least offer an honorarium for each group or performer.
- Find a variety of musical acts or musicians from different genres. Entertainment can be "infotainment" as well, so learning about a new genre should be a learning goal.

- Make sure you have a private venue. Set up tables and chairs; try to have some spotlighting on the performers. Keep the rest of the room dark. Give it some real atmosphere.
- Have free, self-serve coffee.
- Keep the performances relatively short, 45–50 minutes, and allow for some audience Q&A, if the musicians are willing. This will give the audience a chance to know more about the musicians as well as their musical styles.
- Check with local universities or colleges for student performers, who might work for less and who might relate best to younger audiences.
- Advertise through social networking, Facebook, Meetup, and the library's website.

Do not forget to make the performers know how grateful you are, not only through monetary reward but also through promoting their work at the library. They will be more likely to do a second show when you need it.

Engaging New Adults with New or Aspiring Readers

Engaging big brothers or sisters with their younger siblings in a story hour or other program could offer many benefits, for participants and libraries alike. Involving those newly graduated teen advisory board members in storytelling activities could be a means of keeping them enthused about the library as they start to slip away.

Learning goals:

- Learn from those that they look up to, other than parents and grandparents
- Become aware that learning is a lifelong process
- Learn new stories and improve reading skills
- See that reading is cool

Steps to take:

- Start with former teens who were involved with library programs or on a teen advisory board.
- Look into any nearby library science programs where students would be interested in participating.
- Keep these emerging adults involved by presenting a storytelling program as a win-win for the children who are learning to read and the presenters.

• Offer up a special program for siblings, cousins, or other relatives, if there is interest.

CONCLUSION

Our current societal demand for higher education and consequent delayed entry into the workforce, marriage, and starting a family has created a new generation of library users, that of the emerging adult, or the portion of the population caught between high school and adult responsibilities. While this millennial generation has a tendency to drift away from some library services, they still have specific information needs, based mainly in career preparation, and they need a little downtime, too. It is the mission of every local public library to serve its entire community, which includes those digital natives who might be viewed as not needing what the library has to offer. By providing services and programming that will help fill the information need, and even some of the social needs, of this demographic, libraries can remain viable resources for emerging adults. The local library can be there for them in this important transition from "teen advisory board member" to perhaps "adult services board member."

CHAPTER 3

Taking Center Stage: Age Group 25–30

The older group of millennials, ages 25–30, are people who are truly ready to "take center stage," to step out into the spotlight of the job market or the work place and, hopefully, shine. We all know that it sometimes takes several entrances from stage right to finally take the spotlight, but many of us try for the first time at this point in life. We have just finished up with an undergrad or graduate degree program or have been working at our craft for a few years, and we have gotten kind of good at it, so we are ready to strut our stuff! And while we are at it, we might be strutting our stuff in other ways, through dating, looking for potential partners, looking to score our dream house, and beginning to think about "nesting" and starting families of our own. The local library has played an important role in our lives thus far; what does it have to offer now?

LIBRARY USAGE

According to "Younger Americans' Library Habits and Expectations" by Kathryn Zickuhr, Lee Rainie, and Kristen Purcell (http://libraries .pewinternet.org/2013/06/25/younger-americans-library-services/), like their younger twentysomething counterparts, these older millennials are still more likely to report having used library resources in the past year than older adults, including online and print resources. They have visited a library's website and are *just as likely to have visited a library as older adults*. They value free resources such as free databases, free access to computers and the Internet, books for borrowing, quiet spaces, programs and classes, and job or career resources. This demographic also wants more comfortable spaces in libraries, a broader selection of e-books, separate spaces for different services, apps-based access to library services, and more online services. Being users of technology and aware of online resources in general also makes younger adults more aware of online resources and other services offered up by their local public library. If a person is looking at the library's website, they will find out much more about other services and programs going on at the library!

LIBRARY SERVICES FOR THIS AGE GROUP

People in the throes of trying to start a career, find a partner, buy a house, or just relocate for work can find themselves in quite a bit of upheaval, and a quiet place to have a conversation with like-minded individuals, discuss a book, or read a magazine article sure would be nice. A little help for the budding entrepreneur or direction for the newly graduated MBA would be nice, too. And while we are at it, let us throw in some programs that would beat the bar scene and provide a more intellectual framework for meeting new people or even potential partners.

Engaging Young Entrepreneurs

Some of us tear out of college with a ton of "book learning" and no practical ideas about where to start on our given path and I speak from experience. If starting your own business or inventing the next great gadget is the dream, then some practical guidance might be in order. Librarians are in the unique position to harness reliable information and offer it up in the form of collections or programming. If having a business and entrepreneur library is out of the question for your particular situation, get in touch with local business owners, business organizations, and experts in the field and see if you can get something going in the way of networking or mentoring at the library. Try partnering with local organizations for mentoring and local volunteers to assist with classes, such as the following:

- SCORE: An organization offering free mentoring that connects small business owners and entrepreneurs with volunteer business mentors. The SCORE website offers search capability by zip code to locate local SCORE volunteers. Arrange for a SCORE volunteer to visit the library to either provide advice or simply an overview of what the organization can do. https://www.score.org/mentors
- Partner with local business support organizations such as the local Chamber of Commerce, and host monthly after-work "happy hours" for networking opportunities, finding potential customers, and making new connections.

- Offer classes that will benefit budding entrepreneurs. Classroom instruction will provide not only the means of learning a new searching skill or software but also an opportunity to meet like-minded people with similar business goals and interests.
- Invite a local lawyer to discuss the steps to obtain a U.S. patent or trademark, or put together your own program using information from www.uspto.gov.
- Allow crafters to pitch their products to store owners from the community.

Business and Entrepreneurship Libraries

Kansas City Public Library opened the H&R Block Business and Career Center (KCPLBCC) as a dedicated service center for patrons doing research in the areas of business, entrepreneurship, and career and professional development. While every library does not have the staffing or space for a separate business library, here are a number of resources that KCPLBCC provides access to:

- A collection of business books, including *FORTUNE*'s top 75 business books
- Research databases including A to Z databases: 2.3 million job listings, 30 million business profiles, 1.1 million healthcare professionals, a database that is ideal for sales leads, mailing lists, market research, employment opportunities, finding friends, and relatives, and much more.
- ABI/INFORM Complete includes thousands of full-text journals, dissertations, business and economic periodicals, and country and industry reports. This database provides an excellent picture of company and business trends worldwide.
- Hoover's Company Profiles: Find up-to-date content covering more than 40,000 public and nonpublic companies, 600 industries, and 225,000 key executives. Access in-depth industry analyses, information on a company's location, summary financials, top competitors, top officers, and more.
- Demographics Now: Produce comprehensive business and residential lists as well as detailed demographic reports. Assess business viability; perform market and site location analysis; create sales leads and marketing mailing lists; find potential sponsors and donors to grow a nonprofit; prepare a small business plan; and much more.

- Business Plan Pro is a software program that is useful for outlining business plans.
- Online job searches.
- WinWay Résumé Deluxe on the Center's computers.

Job Now: guides you through the necessary tasks to get a job, including acing the interview, building a resume, and personality and career assessments.

- Learning Express offers practice tests for standardized tests, such as the General Equivalency Diploma (GED) and Law School Admission Test (LSAT), civil service exams, the U.S. citizenship test, and occupational licenses, including practice tests for nurses and paramedics.
- Grant research and writing.
- Access to online databases such as Standard & Poor's Net Advantage, S&P ratings on stocks, bonds, and mutual funds, weekly stock "picks and pans," corporate annual reports and other company data, and Stock Screener to identify the right investments for financial planning.
- Print business newspapers and investor newsletters.
- Weekly print publication, Value Line, covers 3,500 stocks and 1,900 mutual funds on a quarterly basis.
- Consultations, computers, and classes.
- Consultation with a business librarian to discuss your business, career, or financial concerns.
- Computers for center patrons, and the library provides free high-speed wireless Internet access.

The KCPLBCC also offers free classes, such as résumé creation, Internet and software basics, and job search strategies. Here is a recent list of class offerings:

- Microsoft Word Basics
- Computer Class—Computer Basics
- Getting Started with E-Books!
- High School Equivalency Classes (GED)
- Computer Class—Internet Basics
- Computer Basics
- Banking Basics

By trying to incorporate and market at least some of the business reference materials or services listed here into your current collection and services, you can market to budding entrepreneurs or established businesses and create new library users.

Fostering Innovation Development

Television shows and infomercials have recently made the notion of everyday people inventing and patenting products more prevalent than ever before. While corporations have an edge when it comes to research and applying for patents, individuals still come up with innovative ideas, and almost 20,000 patents to individuals were granted in the United States alone in 2014. While everything a person needs to apply for a patent can be found on the U.S. Patent and Trademark Office (USPTO) website, some people will still want a book to guide them through the process. Check the Collection Development and Programs section further in this chapter for books on the patent process.

For those determined to "patent it yourself," the USPTO's Office of Innovation Development has a number of good resources for aspiring inventors on its website at http://www.uspto.gov/learning-and-resources/inventors-entrepreneurs-resources.

Some of the topics you will find there include Patent Process Overview, contact information for the Inventors Assistance Center, information about Pro Bono assistance, information for those truly trying to DIY a patent application, and an inventors' assistance directory by state.

New business owners or budding entrepreneurs starting a business to sell a product or offer a service might want to trademark their particular brand. A trademark allows consumers to distinguish different products and services and encourages trademark owners to provide good quality service and value. Trademarks can be quite valuable, especially well-known trademarks, and trademarking a company logo or slogan can be a good first step toward establishing a small or new business.

For more information about patents and trademarks or to do a patent or trademark search, visit www.uspto.gov and look for books on obtaining patents and trademarks in the following section. Again, if you cannot afford a complete business library to provide all of these services or access to all of the databases and collections, focus on a couple of classes that you could offer and then market heavily to your library users, particularly those fresh-out-of-college or trade school folk!

Assisting Millennials as Caregivers

According to a recent article in the *Washington Post*, millennials also have an increasing responsibility in caring for parents and grandparents.

While the typical caregiver is still a woman in her 50s caring for her aging mother, an estimated 9.5 million millennials now provide this kind of help to ailing parents or elderly grandparents. In "A Shift in Responsibility" (October 26, 2015),Tara Bahrampour suggests that because of smaller families, the need for older women in the family to work full-time, the trend for millennials to live at home, and the millennials' more egalitarian ideas of sharing work with women, the younger caregiver is just as likely to be a younger male as female. The millennial caregiver is about 27 years old, lives with or within 20 minutes of those whom they care for, and works 35 hours a week. Millennials are also more likely to be closer to their parents and relate to them more as friends than the baby boomers did with their own parents, enforcing a sense of responsibility for their well-being as well as a willingness to help out.

Because millennials are so good at resource finding and sharing, it is important to make them aware of all of the health literacy resources the library has to offer as well as the online resources that might make their jobs as caregivers easier and more enjoyable. Millennial caregivers can benefit from the use of e-books and online databases in their roles as caregivers as well as enjoy and share streaming video, music, and online magazines with their charges. Library programs that bridge the generations are also a welcome addition to current library programs. For additional information on resources for caregivers, see Chapter 5.

COLLECTION DEVELOPMENT AND PROGRAMS

Given the millennials' need for structure, team spirit, caregiving, and "maker" tendencies, it seems like DIY books should be somewhere near the top of your list when it comes to developing appealing collections for this demographic. There are tons of "maker" and "life hacks" books on the market now ranging in subject from creating wearable electronics to refurbishing furniture to simple hacks for housekeeping. Even though household tips books have been around for many decades (remember *Hints from Heloise*?), choosing titles with current buzz words will attract the younger generation, and there are sure to be current, legitimate new household hacks in the newer books.

Books for Hackers, Makers, and Caregivers

See what you already have in the collection that could be displayed and marketed, such as books on crafting, cooking, and making car and home repairs. In addition to books about crafting, because that list could go on forever, look for books about the "maker movement" and "life hacks" as well, to add to the collection. Three-dimensional (3D) printing is also a hot topic in the maker movement and in libraries in general, as many libraries now offer 3D printing as a service. For these millennials who are ready to step out into center stage of career, work, and life as adults, consider adding even more to your nonfiction collection. These makers/creators want to know how to do things—all sorts of things. So start with a few books about "making" and "life hacks"; add some business and entrepreneurship materials; and finish with some books on patent and trademarking, just to round out the picture for this maker generation.

- *The Big Book of Maker Skills (Popular Science): Tools and Techniques for Building Great Tech Projects* by Chris Hackett
- *Zero to Maker: Learn (Just Enough) to Make (Just About) Anything* by David Lang
- *Make: The Maker's Manual: A Practical Guide to the New Industrial Revolution* by Paolo Aliverti and Andrea Maietta
- *3D Printing* by Cameron Coward
- *Make: Electronics: Learning through Discovery (Make: Technology on Your Time)* by Charles Platt
- *The Successful Caregiver's Guide* by Rick Lauber
- *Juggling Life, Work, and Caregiving* by Amy Goyer
- *A Promise Kept Inspirational Guide for Family Caregivers* by Bonita Bandaries
- *Art of Tinkering* by Karen Wilkinson and Mike Petrich
- *Patent It Yourself: Your Step-by-Step Guide to Filing at the U.S. Patent Office* by David Pressman and Thomas J. Tuytschaevers
- *Invent It, Sell It, Bank It! Make Your Million-Dollar Idea into a Reality* by Lori Greiner
- *Nolo's Patents for Beginners: Quick and Legal* by David Pressman and Richard Stim
- *Patent Pending in 24 Hours* by Richard Stim
- *How to Fly a Horse: The Secret History of Creation, Invention, and Discovery* by Kevin Ashton
- *The Eureka Factor: Aha Moments, Creative Insight, and the Brain* by John Kounios and Mark Beeman
- *Simple Rules: How to Thrive in a Complex World* by Donald Sull and Kathleen M. Eisenhardt
- *Trademark: Legal Care for Your Business & Product Name* by Stephen Elias and Richard Stim

- *How to Register Your Federal Trademark* by Jacob Tingen
- *Patent, Copyright and Trademark: An Intellectual Property Desk Reference* by Richard Stim

Highlight craft and DIY magazines, both electronic and print, currently in the collection and consider subscribing to new maker magazines like *Electronics Maker* and *Make*, either electronically or in print.

Programming to Engage and More

According to "Training the Millennial Generation: Implications for Organizational Climate" (*E-Journal of Organizational Learning & Leadership* 12, no. 1 (Spring 2014): pp. 47–60), some common characteristics of the millennial generation are as follows:

- Ability to multitask and technologically savvy
- Desire for structure
- Achievement focused
- Team oriented

When I questioned an actual millennial about the types of programs that would bring him to the public library, his answer was basically "programs with real content" or "classes." A fairly recent college graduate, he misses the structure and in-depth information he was able to find in the classroom, which demonstrates the "desire for structure" characteristic listed earlier. He mentioned the need for life skills not taught in the classroom, such as negotiating the purchase of a home or saving and investing. In addition to substantive programs, he misses hanging out with his buddies and holding serious, stimulating conversations about current affairs and life in general—the kind that college students like to have over a beer or a cup of coffee. Based on this actual encounter with an actual millennial and my own reading, here are a few programming ideas that might attract this demographic.

Hot Topics Discussion Group

Sometimes people who have been in school for a couple of decades miss the kind of deep conversations and discussions they used to have with their fellow scholars about, well, anything. So, why not set up a discussion group for new college graduates? You can either allow the group to choose its own topics of discussion or have a set schedule of discussions already dreamed up to get the ball rolling. The sessions could range from current or historical events to philosophical discussions and should ideally take place over steaming cups of coffee or a cold beer, just like "back in the day." Try meeting with younger groups outside the library at a local bar or coffee shop for this type of discussion, all the while promoting other library services or programs within the library. Providing a program that is comfortable, familiar, and intellectually stimulating for new graduates will make them feel welcome and at home.

Act Like an Adult!

This series of programs should focus on all those "adult" and very necessary skills that we never learned in school, like:

- Real estate—tips and tricks for buying your first home (there is much to know)
- Landlord rights/tenant rights
- Finances—making the most of savings and investing
- Food-menu planning and basic cooking skills
- Cleaning and organizing—for everything from the office to the pantry
- Time management—simple steps to freeing up more time for play
- Home improvement—learn how to do simple home repairs (this could be an entire series in itself)
- Purchasing power—getting the best deals all the time
- Take charge of your health now, reap benefits later—give users a taste of yoga, meditation, or an exercise class
- Budgeting for life expenses
- Home decorating and design
- Car repair workshops
- Wedding planning

Anything 101

Take any of the topics listed earlier and turn them into a single, more in-depth multiday series, if you can find a presenter who is willing to commit his or her time to the cause. This "101" approach appeals to the newly graduated, still yearning for a classroom learning situation. As computer literate as most millennials are, they still might need instruction in specific computer software or programs, and they are reputed to be creative and interested in creative projects. Financial and health literacy has been widely promoted in the past few years through various organizations.

With "Anything 101," you are only limited by your imagination and finding a presenter or instructor for the course. Check with your state library, foundations, or other agencies devoted to these specific areas of interest, for grant opportunities or potential presenters. Tap into local experts within your community, or even staff members in the library, who are willing to show off their skills, with the intention of gaining new followers and customers down the road. Word of mouth is sometimes the best advertisement for a local expert.

Culinary Literacy and "Foodies"

Now here is yet another form of literacy that I can completely endorse—culinary literacy!

The Free Library of Philadelphia opened its Culinary Literacy Center in June 2014, and it is helping to change the way Philadelphians think about food, nutrition, and literacy. One of the goals of the Culinary Literacy Center is "to advance literacy in Philadelphia in a unique and innovative way—with a fork and spoon" (https://libwww.freelibrary.org/culinary/about.cfm).

The Culinary Literacy Center functions with a commercial-grade kitchen that serves as a classroom and also as a dining space for the citizens of Philadelphia, providing training through a hands-on lab, teaching math via measuring, reading, and science skills via cooking.

The center offers over 350 classes a year, teaching cooks of all ages. It hosts local chefs, cookbook authors, and food truck owners. They offer programs in butchering, food photography, and an annual conference for SNAP recipients and organizations that provide meals and other services to low-income Philadelphians. How cool is that!

So, even if your library cannot possibly afford to have a kitchen dedicated to culinary literacy, programming for "foodies" would be a big hit for millennials. Invite local chefs to do a demonstration using portable stovetop burners and a tabletop convection oven, but check the library's insurance policy first. Bring in a local wine vendor to discuss wine parings. Have a recipe swap. Invite authors of cookbooks based on regional or local cuisine. Every locality has some, even if it is just a local women's club or church that has published a cookbook. Those ladies (and many gents) have cooking skills to share. Have a cake-decorating class. Partner with local health organizations and dieticians to share their knowledge of nutrition, and find an herbalist who can talk about cooking with herbs. Foods (and beverages) are big with the millennial generation. Beer has a language all its own now, and ordering an adult beverage has become increasing more complex. Culinary literacy opens up a whole new avenue of programming opportunities. A millennial focused cooking program follows under "Detailed Programming Ideas." Bon appetit!

Just for Fun Programming Ideas

Seventy-three percent of millennials consider themselves to be creative and define creativity in a slightly different way than generations past. They tend to think of creativity as also relating to problem-solving skills and play and consequently engage in "maker" activities more often as a whole (http://www.howcoolbrandsstayhot.com/2015/03/17/a-millennial-view-on-creativity/). Think of the renewed interest in knitting, the flourishing of Etsy, the interest in craft beers, and craft coffees and farm to table eateries. They are also more adventurous, wanting to see the world and willing to accept some danger in the process, which is, I feel compelled to say, simply part of youth. All that being said, there are any number of programs, in addition to your literary speed dating program, that would appeal to the creative/maker/excitement junkies of this demographic who might still have some free time on their hands:

- Dedicated maker space to allow for crafting, demonstrating, and making all sorts of things
- Book and film discussions at the local brew pub
- "Maker" projects like silk screening, knitting, woodworking, beer brewing, and coffee roasting
- Comic book hero trivia night
- Pop culture trivia night
- Travel on the cheap
- Cards/poker night
- Adult spelling bee
- Coloring for grown-ups

MORE DETAILED PROGRAMMING IDEAS

Please Judge a Book by Its Cover

Speed dating based on literary tastes has been around for a few years now, but maybe you have not had the nerve or felt the need to try it. Bookstores have hopped on the literary speed dating bandwagon, and many libraries have experienced success with this type of program including San Francisco Public, Fort Collins, Colorado, Chattanooga, Tennessee, and Omaha Public Library. Speed dating programs are an alternative to meeting strangers online, and what could be better than dating based on literary tastes?

Learning goals:

- Get to know people with similar literary tastes and romantic interest.
- Connect with like-minded singles in a safe atmosphere.
- Learn more about genres through talking with others.
- Increase interest in other genres.
- Learn more about other library programs and services.

Steps to take:

- Have individuals register for the event with information, including age, gender, gender dating preference, and favorite reading genre.
- Set the stage with some smooth jazz or romantic music.
- Set up tables for individual five minute "dates."
- Have some snacks and beverages (maybe provided by the culinary literacy class mentioned earlier).

Also display new fiction in every genre, to pique more interest in reading.

Turn people loose and see if any sparks fly! Hopefully, in this instance, participants will be able to judge a book (and its owner) by its cover, and you could end up with a wedding in the stacks!

Keeping Body and Soul Together

This cooking series will focus on simple cooking techniques that many younger adults might not have learned at home. Use several different presenters, if location and budget allow, or find a "hobby chef" in your area. With the advent of food networks and YouTube, hobby chefs are everywhere these days, some of them trying to turn their hobby into a business or career. A little promo work at the library might be the boost that they need.

Learning goals:

- Learn how to cook simple dishes that will ward off starvation.
- Save money on eating out.
- Meet others with similar information needs.
- Learn about relevant library collections.

Steps to take:

- Locate local "chefs" through home extension services, local businesses, or word of mouth.
- Have a budget and offer some sort of honorarium.
- If the library is not equipped with a kitchen, electric burners and skillets can be used.
- Ensure that each demonstration is simple, focusing on staple dishes.
- Work with local restaurants to supply food for the presentation.
- Limit the number of participants and allow for "tasting portions" only.
- Think of having a three-part series, which includes two simple breakfast dishes, packable lunch ideas, and two easy dinner recipes.
- Check with administration regarding insurance coverage—very important.
- Have a supply of disposable service ware for tasting purposes.

While a program like this might seem riskier than some, cooking and food preparation are increasingly popular subjects with the general population, and younger library users might need some assistance in this area. If these budding chefs graduate from basic training, future offerings of specialty dishes might be in order!

Book Discussions outside the Library

While anyone can hold a book discussion in the library, it takes a bit of doing to sponsor book discussion groups *outside* the library and could draw the interest of the 25–30 age group. Accustomed to "hanging out" and discussing all kinds of issues during the secondary education years, millennials might be more likely to have a book discussion in a quiet corner of a local brewery (beer is big now) or coffee house, drawing them back into the fold some of those former teen library users.

Learning goals:

- Engage in finding new topics of interest through reading.
- Meet others with like interests in similar demographic.
- Expand understanding and knowledge of the chosen book through discussion.

Steps to take:

- Contact local coffee houses or breweries about the proposition.
- Emphasize the community benefit of partnering with the library.
- Choose a time when the venue is not normally crowded.
- Set up some ground rules for participants.
- Try to gauge interest through social media like Facebook and Meetup.
- Choose two or three titles and allow interested parties to narrow it down to one.
- Provide copies of books for checkout.
- Come up with discussion questions to "prime the pump."
- Be prepared to participate, if people become suddenly shy.

Discussion groups do not necessarily have to focus on books but could extend to topics ranging from current events to climate change. Be prepared to referee if discussions become too heated; bring along a flyer or talk up something interesting and new at the library.

CONCLUSION

The older millennial generation while still maintaining many of the characteristics of younger emerging adults have different information needs and often greater responsibilities than their younger counterparts. As they approach the age of 30, they will most likely have to settle into a workplace and learn how to play by at least some of the rules. They are also more likely to also share in the responsibility of caring for an older relative. This can also be the time in which they might begin to think of settling down with a mate and begin the long climb into independence. Libraries can assist them with job searching, career and entrepreneurial desires and needs, and information about and assistance with caregiving through digital resources and programs. Libraries can also offer a comfortable place to try out new ideas, take a class, hold book and hot topic discussions, and enjoy game nights, allowing them to be "adultolescents" for just a little bit longer.

CHAPTER 4

Settling Down: Age Group 30–40

I f a person has not already "settled down," the approach of the big "3-0" is usually enough to make one think about it long and hard, anyway. It is no wonder that I finally got married at the age of 30. There is something about this decade that says to us, "Hey, time to settle down. Put those dancing shoes away. Pick your clothes up off the floor. Find a better place to live. Get a job. Grow up." Maybe it is the first hint of crow's feet around our fragile eye area that makes us realize we have got to do something-fast!!

While many women are choosing not to have children at all, statistics show that among women between age 25 and 29, 49.6 percent were childless in 2014, but for women between age 30 and 34, that number dropped to 28.9 percent, meaning that among those who do choose to have children, more women are delaying the birth of their first child (http://time.com/3774620/more-women-not-having-kids/). With this sort of delay in starting a family, this stage in life can find many of us trying to balance career and young children, already worrying about saving for the kids' college fund, making home improvements or looking for a bigger place to house the growing family.

The 30s seems to be the decade in which we finally realize that we have to be more practical or suffer the consequences later. According to the U.S. Census Bureau, home ownership almost doubles from the decade of our 20s to the decade of our 30s (https://www.census.gov/housing/hvs/data/charts/fig07.pdf), proof positive of the "settling down" theme of this stage in life. Blogs and magazine articles geared toward this slightly more mature audience seem to revolve around very practical themes upon which you can focus when looking at programming and collection development. While career and finding the "perfect fit" in the workplace might haunt some of us forever (Stop pointing at me!), usually at some point in our 30s, we realize we have got to bring home the bacon and oftentimes extra bacon, if there are other mouths to feed on the horizon. In various "what to do in your 30s" blogs, some of the main themes are as follows:

- Saving for the future
- Buying a house
- Health care
- Honing skills or professional expertise
- More focus on family and good friends
- Travel
- Self-acceptance
- Partnering and marriage
- Adopting or having children
- Getting a pet

These are all very grown-up themes and almost all of them require funding, which ultimately leads to holding down a job. As in any stage of life, libraries offer unique resources in the form of collections, both print and electronic, informational programs, research assistance, and online tools to help make some of the challenges of settling down easier. By building programs and collections around these themes, libraries can help to smooth the transition from "adultolescent" into real adult.

LIBRARY SERVICES FOR THIS AGE GROUP

Not that other age groups do not enjoy online services (because we know they do) this age group, the young parent, or the more settled young adult can really appreciate online services provided by the local library, such as free online magazines, music, e-books, and video.

In *Stepping into the Stream: Bringing Netflix-style Video to Libraries*, Stephanie Klose writes that libraries sometimes have as difficult a time marketing online services as onsite programs and services. The most popular video services offered by vendors include Midwest Tape's hoopla, OverDrive's streaming service, LibraryIdeas's Freegal Movies and Television, and IndieFlix, which is distributed to libraries by Recorded Books. A quiet Friday evening at home in one's jammies with a streaming video can be just the thing after a long hectic work week, or once the kids have been put to bed.

In addition to the library website, use social networking as a means to make sure that these online offerings are known to young parents or working young adults. Library users do not always have to come into the library to reap the benefits of the services we offer (http://reviews .libraryjournal.com/2014/04/media/video/stepping-into-the-stream -bringing-netflix-style-video-to-libraries/).

COLLECTION DEVELOPMENT AND PROGRAMS

At this stage in the game, even though a person can find a video on just about how to do anything, sometimes it is good to have many "how tos" in one place. That is the beauty of books. When I worked in archives for several years, I would pull out the biggest volume I could find to show to school tours. I would always say, "This looks like a crazy idea, doesn't it? Why would anyone want to make a book that weights 25 lbs. and takes up half a 6 foot table?"

"Because it is a convenient way to keep lots of information together in one place," I would reply to myself, and that was exactly the function these books, usually registers of some sort, served. They kept many pages of records neatly together, in one place.

This is the same concept for books on home and car repair, drugs and drug interactions, cookbooks, crafting books, childcare books, and so on. Unless a person knows of reliable resources on the web, it is usually safer to consult a book about things that are of real importance. Having a strong collection of "how to" books is a good choice for these newly minted adults.

Make sure that your library collection includes the following:

- Newer cookbooks, such as *The Food Lab: Better Home Cooking through Science* by J. Kenji López-Alt, *Fix-It and Forget-It Big Cookbook: 1400 Best Slow Cooker Recipes!* by Phyllis Good, and some celebrity cooks books, like *The Barefoot Contessa Cookbook* by Ina Garten, and *Cooking Like a Master Chef: 100 Recipes to Make the Everyday Extraordinary* by Graham Elliot
- Urban homesteading books, such as *Urban Homesteading: Heirloom Skills for Sustainable Living* by Rachel Kaplan, *The Urban Homestead: Your Guide to Self-Sufficient Living in the Heart of the City* by Kelly Koyne, and *A Chicken in Every Yard: The Urban Farm Store's Guide to Chicken Keeping* by Robert Litt and Hannah Litt
- Books on keeping a home, such as *The Hands-On Home: A Seasonal Guide to Cooking, Preserving & Natural Homekeeping* by Erica Strauss and *The Year of Cozy: 125 Recipes, Crafts, and Other Homemade Adventures by* Adrianna Adarme

- Books on easy entertaining such as *Food with Friends: The Art of Simple Gatherings* by Leela Cyd, *Best Game Day Recipes* by Diana Loera, and *Occasional Drinking: The Best Wines and Beers to Pair with Every Situation That Calls for a Drink* by Diane McMartin
- Books on pet care like, such as *The Ultimate Encyclopedia of Small Pets & Pet Care* by David Alderton and *Total Dog Manual: Meet, Train and Care for Your New Best* by The Editors of Adopt-a-Pet.com and David Meyer
- Newer books on parenting, like *The Rabbit Who Wants to Fall Asleep: A New Way of Getting Children to Sleep* by Carl-Johan Forssén Ehrlin and Irina Maununen, *How to Raise an Adult: Break Free of the Overparenting Trap and Prepare Your Kid for Success* by Julie Lythcott-Haims, and the *What to Expect…*books
- Pregnancy and baby names
- Books on date night ideas, such as *Date Night In: More than 120 Recipes to Nourish Your Relationship* by Ashley Rodriguez and *Dating Fun for Couples: 400 creative dating ideas for you to try* by Jensen, PhD, Vern A.
- Books for couples, such as local nature getaways, hiking, beaches, camping
- Urban adventures within driving distance
- Nearby bed and breakfast, spa getaway and winery guides

Constant "Googling" for bits and pieces on different subjects can become tiresome. Having a book that allows for a broader and more definitive understanding of gardening, or home repair, or any other subject of choice just makes sense.

Programming with Couples in Mind

I can honestly say that I have not seen much programming presented with couples in mind in libraries and I thought this was a great idea on the part of one of my contributors, who kindly helped me come up with some ideas to bring couples, married or not, with our without children, into the library:

- Learning couples massage
- Couples only vacation planning
- Romantic getaways, including LGBT friendly hotspots
- Couples cooking class
- He said/she said book club

- LGBT couples book club
- Gender-based Communication Skills
- Dance classes
- Date night at the library with wine tasting (with kids in story hour, optional)
- Gardening, canning, and other "homesteading" skills
- Programs featuring local songwriters/musicians

Many of these programs will require outside help, unless you have a massage therapist or dance instructor on staff. Often local musicians, instructors, or craftspeople will donate their time to the library for an opportunity to show off their skills and talent and build a loyal following. If budget is a problem, it never hurts to ask. Consider offering licensed childcare at these programs to encourage couples (or any adults) to attend by freeing them from the chore and expense of finding child care services. Remember that grant opportunities for educational programs are also readily available. Check with local foundations or your state library for funding opportunities.

No Kidding?

Since there are sure to be library users or would-be library users in this age group in your community who have not yet "settled down" or who have decided not to have children or even forego the conventional marriage route, it would behoove any smart librarian to have programs and collections that appeal to this demographic. These are the very people you might lose as lifelong library users, so do not ignore them! Single parents, DINKS (Double Income No Kids), and SINKS (Single Income No Kids—I just made that up) who are settling into careers, buying homes or just testing out being grown-up and on their own can still find useful information and programs through the local library.

Do Not Forget the Fur Babies!

People of all ages have and love their fur babies, but according to Quartz Media in an article written by Roberto A. Ferdman, "Americans are having dogs instead of babies" purports that the drop in the number of younger women having babies has also resulted in an increase in the number of younger women owning small dogs (http://qz.com/197416/americans -are-having-dogs-instead-of-babies/). While this may not be entirely the cause of the rise in pet ownership, we all know many people who are completely devoted to their fur babies. Whether they are cat people or dog people or trans-species, pet owners seem to have become increasingly devoted and vocal about their devotion. Cat ladies are no longer ashamed. Facebook feeds are filled with pictures of pooches. Promoting collections about caring for pets and maybe even offering a program or two could be a good way to reach out to younger adults who might be settling down with a furry friend as the smallest member of their household.

If the library has access to an outdoor space, have an outdoor event for dog owners. If you have a good vacuum cleaner with a Hepa filter, you might even allow pet owners to bring their bundles of fluff into an enclosed space for a special event, like a pet fashion show or allow the knitting club to share knit fashions for pets. Consider sponsoring an event at a location outside the library, if necessary, just to avoid any complaints about allergies, but do not ignore the burgeoning devotion to furry friends!

Pets are increasingly allowed into designated "pet patios" at restaurants and I have even seen an ad for a "cat café," especially for cat owners and their kitties. There is no denying that Americans love their pets and seem to be asking for pet acceptance in more and more places. While you might not be ready to have "Fur Babies at the Library Day," a cat or dog themed book club might attract the die-hard pet lovers and turn them into die-hard library fans. While you are at it, go ahead and get these two titles for your collection:

Knitting with Dog Hair: Better a Sweater from a Dog You Know and Love than from a Sheep You'll Never Meet by Kendall Crolius and Anne Montgomery

Crafting with Cat Hair: Cute Handicrafts to Make with Your Cat by Kaori Tsutaya and Amy Hirschman

In addition to the programming suggestions mentioned earlier, you might also consider the following:

- Having an obedience training expert offer classes
- A pet adoption program
- Making pet fashions and costumes, including knitting for pets or knitting with pet hair
- DIY pet foods and toys
- Pet Grooming 101

Think about promoting your programs at pet stores, shelters, and dog parks and be prepared to get these fur baby parents interested in everything the library has to offer them!

LIBRARY SERVICES FOR CHILDREN

"What's this doing here?" you might be thinking. As it turns out educating the parents of small children about early literacy development is an important tool in a child's intellectual development and growth. Consequently, library services to small children can be very important to the "settling down" demographic, as this is the time in which young parents are most likely to bring their children into the library to check out books and attend programs. As it just so happens, this is a most important time in a child's development. There are numerous programs being implemented in libraries and through nonprofit organizations that offer "first books" to infants, or books for daycares where small children spend their time away from home, particularly in low-income or high-immigrant population areas.

Statewide Programs for Children

The California State Library has sponsored a statewide initiative since 2006, in the form of Library Services and Technology Act (LSTA) grants to library jurisdictions around the state to implement family-focused, early learning programs and services. Early Learning with Families (ELF) supports the ongoing evolution of library services to young children (age up to five), their families and caregivers.

Through ELF, some California libraries have reorganized collections, created welcoming spaces, and offered developmentally appropriate programs for young children and their families. By partnering with local organizations that share similar childhood literacy goals, these libraries have been able to leverage and expand this important work. According to the ELF section of the California State Library's website "up until 4th grade, children are essentially learning to read but from 4th grade on they are reading to learn. Children who don't read at grade level by the end of 3rd grade are four times more likely not to graduate from high school than more proficient readers. According to the 2013 National Assessment of Educational Progress, 47% of these low performing students come from low-income families."

What predicts 3rd grade reading levels? The number of words a child knows by the time he or she is two to three years old! Yet as early as 18 months, low-income children begin to fall behind in vocabulary development. They tend to:

- have few, if any, books in the home;
- hear as many as 30 million fewer words than their more affluent peers by age four; and

- by age 5, many recognize only 9 letters of the alphabet compared to a typical middle-class child who recognizes 22 letters.

This is an astonishingly sad statistic, but by engaging parents to read with their preschoolers, children can learn more and new words, and consequently become better readers later on. According to the ELF project web page, "A large and growing body of research provides persuasive evidence confirming the particular importance of these first years in the development of a child's brain. During this time, neural connections are established that provide the foundation for language, reasoning, problem solving, social skills, behavior and emotional health .... Everything a child sees, touches, tastes, smells or hears helps to shape the brain for thinking, feeling, moving, and learning. When children have high-quality early learning experiences they are better prepared to succeed in school and in life." How wonderful is that? (http://elf2.library.ca.gov/why/literacy.html)

Often with young children, mommy and daddy find themselves working and paying another adult to care for preschool-age children while parents work. Many of the young children brought to storytime at the library are accompanied by paid caregivers and in some areas, particularly urban areas, the caregivers could be new Americans, lacking the skills necessary to deliver reading fundamentals to young children. Programming devoted to caregivers is in many ways just as important as those provided to the children themselves. Or programs that provide benefits to both the caregiver and the child (family literacy models) can serve as a tremendous resource to these demographics. See the chapter on outreach to special populations for more on this subject, as well as the family literacy section of this chapter.

FAMILY LITERACY

In "Just Good Practice" (Public Libraries, 2015), Dorothy Stoltz, Paula Isett, Linda Zang, Liza Trye, and Liz Sundermann describe several successful family literacy programs through partnerships of the Maryland State Department of Education, public libraries, and early literacy groups in the state of Maryland.

One such program is the Read and Play program, demonstrating to young parents how to read, sing, and play with a newborn. The Library Family Café discussion group is focused on learning topics and can be tailored to a community's needs. Some libraries use activity play stations, while others use the Every Child Ready to Read (ECRR) format, discussed in the next section. The Library Family Café model can take children from infancy to formal education, with parents learning along the way.

Family Info Center can be found in one or two branches of every library system, and provides information specific to early literacy, early learning, and community partners in these areas. Local early childhood organizations share their literature through the library, in addition to the library's pamphlets and handouts on early learning and literacy.

The article offers up four tenets of engaging families, reminding parents that they are a child's first teacher, that the public library is a resource for family learning, that library staff are trained to assist early learning, and that libraries function best as providers of early learning activities when they partner with caregivers, and community agencies and organizations, capitalizing on concerted community efforts.

In The Maryland Early Childhood Family Engagement Framework published by the Maryland Family Engagement Coalition, there are seven common goals listed that all partners in early childhood education, including libraries, can embrace to develop good strategies for achieving goals. As stated in The Framework, "Family engagement practices must be initiated and implemented with clear goals in mind." These goals are as follows:

Goal 1: Family engagement initiatives should promote family well-being.

Maryland's vision for family engagement is a two-generation strategy. Families are the key to a child's early development and learning. As such, a goal of family engagement initiatives must be to support family well-being. Maryland's family engagement initiatives and the family engagement practices of early care and education providers should promote the safety, health, and financial security of families so that they can successfully parent their young children.

Goal 2: Family engagement initiatives should promote positive parent-child relationships.

Research clearly documents the link between competent parenting, strong parent-child bonds, and positive school readiness outcomes. Given the importance of parent-child relationships, it is imperative that Maryland's family engagement initiatives and the practices of early care and education providers have the goal, beginning with the transition to parenthood, of supporting parents and families in developing warm relationships that nurture their child's learning and development. This begins with developing warm, nurturing relationships among adults, including between staff members, and between staff and parents and other adult family members.

Goal 3: Family engagement initiatives should support families as life-long educators of their children.

Parents and family members are their child's first teachers. Maryland initiatives and the practices of early care and education providers should create collaborative relationships with a variety of service entities to support and empower the family in its role as first teacher.

Goal 4: Family engagement initiatives should support the educational aspirations of parents and families.

Research has documented the link between parental education—particularly maternal education levels—and positive school readiness outcomes. When parents and other adults in the family strive to achieve their educational goals, they become a positive example to their children regarding the importance of education. Therefore, a goal of Maryland initiatives and the practices of early care and education providers should be to support parents and families to advance their own interests through education, training, and other experiences that support their parenting, careers, and life goals.

Goal 5: Family engagement initiatives should support families through the care and education transitions of early childhood.

When a child transitions to a new early care and education provider, or to the formal education system, the child and family changes setting, teacher, and learning culture. These transitions are challenging for parents and families— and often for providers and teachers—to navigate. Therefore, Maryland initiatives and the practices of early care and education providers should support families as they make transitions with their children to new learning environments.

Goal 6: Family engagement initiatives should connect families to their peers and to the community.

Personal networks are a key source of support for families with young children. Learning from one another and sharing common experiences can inform parents and families about resources, expand parenting strategies, and offer a source of comfort. Maryland initiatives and the family engagement practices of early care and education providers should support parents and families to form connections with peers and mentors in formal or informal social networks that are supportive and that enhance social well-being and community life.

Goal 7: Family engagement initiatives should support the development of families as leaders and child advocates.

When parents and families are empowered, they can be a strong force for positive change in their child's education and in many other areas of life. Therefore, Maryland initiatives and the family engagement practices of early care and education providers should support families to participate in leadership development, decision-making, program policy development, and community and state organizing activities to improve children's development and learning experiences.

The entire document also includes strategies for early care and education providers to meet the goals set forth, such as the following:

Welcome all families—and all family structures, sizes, and arrangements.

- Initiate relationships with families that are receptive, responsive, and respectful.
- Include family-friendly spaces with pictures and materials that affirm, welcome and accept all families.
- Engage in honest dialogue with families about their expectations and staff/program objectives.
- Hold the child and family in high regard and partner effectively with all parents.
- Provide opportunities that support parents' needs to connect with other parents for reflection, information, ideas, and support.
- Support parent-child relationships in a way that values the culture and language of the family and recognizes how cultural influences impact family development.
- Welcome families to observe and participate in their child's classroom or home-based activities.
- Support and encourage parents to share tips on everyday learning practices with staff and other families.
- Make information available that supports adults' personal growth and career development.

In implementing programs for early and family literacy, libraries everywhere can adapt and use these goals and strategies as part of an implementation plan.

Every Child Ready to Read

Every Child Ready to Read (ECRR) is a parent education program in public libraries. It began as a "partnership of the Public Library Association (PLA) and Association for Library Service to Children (ALSC) to allow public libraries to have an even greater impact on early literacy through focusing on educating parents and caregivers" (http://www.everychildreadytoread.org/about). By teaching the primary adults in a child's life about the importance of early literacy and how to nurture prereading skills at home, the child has a greater chance of being successful in reading and school, when formal training begins. This is the basis of Every Child Ready to Read @ your library. A program that has been in libraries since 2004, the focus on educating parents and caregivers is a different approach for many libraries and has proven its value since its inception. By offering early literacy services to children of young parents, the library is ultimately providing services to children and their young parents.

PRIME TIME, Inc.

PRIME TIME is another family literacy program, which brings young parents and children into the library. Created by the Louisiana Endowment for the Humanities (LEH) in 1991, the original program, PRIME TIME Family Reading Time, was an "award-winning reading, discussion, and storytelling series based on illustrated children's books .... The program helped low-income, low-literate families bond around the act of reading and talking about books. It modeled and encouraged family reading and discussion of humanities topics, and aided parents and children in selecting books and becoming active public library users" (http://www.ala.org/programming/primetime/primetimefamily). In its current incarnation, PRIME TIME, Inc. still partners with libraries and other service organizations to carry out its purpose. In 2011, PRIME TIME, Inc. released these statistics in "Stemming the Tide of Intergenerational Illiteracy: A Ten-Year Impact Study of PRIME TIME FAMILY READING TIME" (http://primetimefamily.org/program-impact/#sthash.6kRo6gJJ.dpuf):

- More than 6,900 individuals completed the program
- Family retention rate across programs was 94.2 percent
- Twenty-three percent weekly and 17.2 percent monthly increase in public library use among participants
- A positive change in attitude toward library use was reported by 78.5 percent participants
- Daily reading frequency as a family was increased by 8.1 percent
- Eighty-five percent participants reported increase in positive family interactions, or bonding, improving reading attitudes and behaviors
- A positive change in attitude toward reading was reported by 80.4 percent participants

- Increase in discussion participation among the adults was observed by 77.5 percent
- Eighty-five percent observed increase in discussion participation among the children

PRIME TIME also contributes to the continuation of the family reading experience by focusing on children ages 3–10. This program also leans more heavily on discussion of humanities-related issues found in the stories, which makes it ideal for families with older children. Read more of the impact study at http://primetimefamily.org/program-impact/#sthash.6kRo6gJJ.dpuf.

Paws for Reading

Paws for Reading is a particular program offered in some northeastern states, sponsored by a number of foundations and businesses, which allows children who struggle with reading to read to a trained service animal. From the Paws for Reading website:

> PAWS for Reading is a program that allows children to read aloud to a therapy dog (or cat, or bunny!) in order to improve reading and communication skills. Children read individually to trained therapy pets (and their handlers) in schools, libraries, or other settings where they can feel comfortable and confident—and have fun! After all, a dog will not correct them or make them feel awkward if they stumble. http://www.pawsforpeople.org/children/paws-for-reading/

While this particular program may be out of reach for your library, similar models are offered all around the country. Offering a similar program, or an educational program in which parents and children at least learn about reading to their pets at home, might be an option for you.

1,000 Books before Kindergarten

Another important program for parents with small children is 1,000 Books before Kindergarten. According to an article by Beth Crist, Youth and Family Services Consultant at the Colorado State Library:

> The program is based upon solid evidence from research findings that the more children ages 0–5 hear books read to them, the more

prepared they will be to learn to read upon reaching kindergarten.
https://www.cde.state.co.us/cdelib/1000booksprogramtoolkit

Libraries administer the program differently, but the general framework is based upon the summer reading program model of encouraging and rewarding reading with incentives. Parents of children 0–5 sign up for the program at their public library, although a few elementary schools in the Midwest offer the program too.

Libraries provide the parents with reading logs to track how many books they and others read to their children. Some libraries give small incentives when the families reach certain reading milestones, like 50 books. When the families have reached 1,000 books before the child reaches kindergarten, they have successfully completed the program.

Besides having children hear 1,000 before kindergarten, program goals may include

- ensuring kids enter kindergarten ready to read,
- having an opportunity to present parents with information about early literacy,
- instilling the lifelong love of reading in young children,
- fostering a positive connection to the library for families and children,
- reinforcing parents' role as their child's first and best teachers, and
- creating a network of families and children that are committed to literacy and education.

Cost and Maintenance

The model is really flexible and can be started and maintained with very little to a lot of funding. An inexpensive program might look like this:

Upon registration, the family receives a simple reading log designed in-house, a list of recommended books in your collection appropriate for the child's age, info for the parents on early literacy, and info about the library including a library card application and a schedule of storytimes and other children's programs.

After reading 25 or 50 books, the family receives a sticker on the reading log, or a bookmark. They may also get to put an item (a paper animal, star, etc.) with the child's name on a bulletin board made for the program.

After reading 250 or 500 books, the family receives a free book to keep, and upon completing the program, the family receives a certificate and is invited to attend a once-a-year congratulations party for everyone who has finished that year; simple refreshments or more substantial fare like pizza donated by local restaurants are served, and craft time is offered.

With more funding, other items may be included like the following: Upon registration, the family receives a canvas book bag with reading log sheets in a binder, an age-appropriate book and toy, info for the parents on early literacy, and info about the library including a library card application, a schedule of storytimes and other children's programs, and a list of recommended books for the child's age in your collection. Other incentives may be offered more frequently and could include free books, educational toys, music CDs, puppets, puzzles, coloring books, crayons, and so on. The annual party may include all participants with special recognition given to the "graduates."

Parents can track reading either by recording each title or checking a box/filling in a shape to indicate one book read (the latter option may be more beneficial for parents with low literacy or low English literacy). A few libraries that offer the program allow each title to be entered only once, even if it is read over and over, but most allow parents to include the title each time they read it. Parents can include books that their children hear in library storytimes, in preschool, from other family members, and elsewhere too. If a family has more than one child enrolled in the program and someone reads the same book to all of them, all get to count the book.

While it is best for parents to join the program just after their child is born, most libraries offering the program allow them to begin any time before their child enters kindergarten.

A good way for parents to think about it is this: if they read only one book at bedtime every night for three years, they will have read 1095 books! If they read 3 books a day, they will read 1095 books in only one year! If they begin when their child is first born and read just 4 books per week, they will have read 1040 by the time the child reaches kindergarten.

Options to enhance the program may be used, such as the following:

- Producing a quarterly newsletter (and/or blog about the program) for all parents registered to help keep families engaged in the program and to allow another opportunity to distribute early literacy.
- Using tips, book lists, your storytime schedule, and fun activities.
- Having a quarterly meeting of all families registered, which serves as a way to build a community.
- Networking amongst families, as well as another time to impart early literacy info. Inviting other relevant community organizations

can help families learn of other services available to them, and can help the library build partnerships.

- Partnering with preschools, daycares, schools, nonprofits, social service agencies, Early Childhood Councils, and other organizations to cross promote services and offer joint programs.
- Seeking sponsors in local businesses for cash and in-kind contributions (sponsors can give to the program as a whole or can sponsor one child or family) as well as seeking funding from nonprofits and foundations.
- Tying the program into your summer reading program.
- Engaging great volunteers to assist with program promotion, maintaining registrant info, reading to children, and so on.
- Initiating the program with a community baby shower for parents-to-be and signing them up for the program before their child even arrives (and this could be an annual event to attract new families to the program).

Many of these great suggestions from the Colorado State Library can work with any family literacy program. Design your own program and make use of any pieces/parts that would work in your community.

OTHER KINDS OF LITERACY

People use libraries for all of their literacy needs and in addition to helping library users improve their information literacy skills, we can offer programming in any number of areas and improve the literacy levels in different subject areas.

Financial Literacy

Financial literacy has been a popular topic for programming in libraries for some time, and the need for financial literacy continues, with volatile financial markets at home and abroad occurring on a regular basis. The Institute of Museum and Library Services (IMLS) awarded a Laura Bush 21st Century Librarian Grant to the New York Public Library (NYPL) in 2011 for Money Matters, designed to educate librarians about financial reference tools, in order to better serve the public. After the initial training period, in which over 250 library workers participated, much of the training materials needed to conduct workshops in the area of financial literacy remain on a website, creating an opportunity to benefit from the body of knowledge and information created by this IMLS funded collaboration. Access to training curriculum in areas like banking, credit, investing, identity theft, income taxes, and retirement planning can be found at Money Matter$ Pro (https://sites.google.com/a/nypl.org/money-matters/home/curriculum).

Financial Literacy Resources Online

Consumer.Gov written in very simple language was developed by the Federal Trade Commission (FTC) and offers the basics of understanding money, credit, banking, scams, and more (http://www.consumer.gov).

Money as You Grow, created by the President's Advisory Council on Financial Capability, is a website highlighting the 20 essential lessons kids need to learn about money. It divides up the lessons per age group and includes a downloadable poster (http://www.moneyasyougrow.org).

Smart Investing @ Your Library, a partnership between the FINRA Investor Education Foundation and the American Library Association, not only offers grant opportunities for public libraries to enhance their financial literacy programming but also provides great resources and tools to download and share with patrons (http://smartinvesting.ala.org/).

Participate in Money Smart Week @ your library, a national initiative between the ALA and the Federal Reserve Bank (Chicago) to provide financial literacy programming to help members of your community better manage their personal finances (http://www.ala.org/offices/money-smart-week).

A 529 College Savings Plan is an education savings plan operated by a state or educational institution. A 529 plan allows families to set aside funds for future college costs and allow the savings to grow tax-free, either through an automatic monthly contribution or an annual gift. 529 plan funds can be used for many of the peripheral educational expenses such as computers, books, and relevant equipment. Even living expenses are eligible for funding through a 529 plan as long as the student is attending college at least half time. A list of 529 College Savings Plans is listed by state at savingforcollege.com (http://www.savingforcollege.com/enroll_in_a_529_plan/).

By using these resources, programming ideas, and learning from online tutorials and trainings, you can, in turn, tailor programs to your own library needs, or simply point library users to valuable resources online, in order to meet these young and enterprising adults financial information needs.

Health Literacy

Parents of young children, caregivers, garden variety hypochondriacs (Stop pointing at me!), and everyday people of all ages need access to reliable health information, but sometimes young parents need special reassurance about their child's health. Health literacy trainings and programs are a great option for most demographics, but tailoring some programs specifically for parents of young children is a programming idea that I do not see very often. For several years while working as a consultant for the Missouri State Library, I worked with the state liaison to the National Network of Libraries of Medicine (NNLM) to bring health literacy training to librarians around the state. Since the NNLM is a national network, there are most likely trainers in your state or region who could assist you and your staff with becoming better health literacy librarians. The NNLM website lists regional libraries and liaisons at http://nnlm.gov.

Trainings by the NNLM focus on Federal resources like MedLine and MedLine Plus, PubMed, the Center for Disease Control, ToxNet, and Household Products Database. These trusted resources can supply anxious parents and nonparents alike, as well as younger caregivers and the newly responsible adult with reliable medical information at their fingertips, if they know about them and know how to use them. That is where you come in, dear librarian.

MORE DETAILED PROGRAMMING IDEAS

Pet Grooming 101

With fur babies sometimes serving as "place holders" until couples decide to obtain a real baby, either through traditional methods or adoption, having a program for those lovable four-footed babies can be a win-win-win for the pets, the library, and the owners. While programs suggested earlier might appeal more to women, knitting pet clothes, fur baby fashion show, a generic grooming program would be attractive to anyone.

Learning goals:

- Learn how to better care for pets
- Increase the health and well-being of furry friends through good hygiene
- Save a bit of money on the groomers
- Learn more about library services and other programs

Steps to take:

- Contact local pet-grooming shops and find a couple of willing presenters, for dogs and cats
- Allow the groomers to bring their own "models" for this program
- Have a budget and offer at least an honorarium
- Focus on the simplest of grooming techniques, bathing, trimming, nail clipping, nothing fancy
- Emphasize that the groomers will be reaching new audiences and hopefully gaining new customers
- Set up can best be determined by the groomers, but a tub for washing and one for rinsing would probably be needed
- Advertise any other pet related programs
- Bring in some pet-grooming books, and point to any e-books available

As with the cooking demonstration in Chapter 3, programs with pets can be a little riskier but might well offer a greater reward. Check your insurance policy, schedule a private space for the program, and advertise through social media and pet-related local businesses. It is always a good idea to throw something a little different into the programming mix!

Buying Your First Home

Buying a house is intimidating and costly. Some people never own a home for these reasons, and others prefer to rent. But the dream of home ownership is part and parcel of the all-American dream, and younger people looking to settle down and start a family are frequently in the market for home ownership.

Learning goals:

- Weighing the benefits of buying or renting
- What to look for in your investment in a property
- Learn about any government resources for new home owners
- Calculating down payments and other costs in buying
- Shopping for a mortgage
- When and how to negotiate or at least ask your realtor

Steps to take:

- Consider making this program a panel discussion
- Involve realtors from different types of agencies, such as those that offer minimal assistance to full-service agencies

- Involve a local lending agency
- Do some research and provide a segment on online mortgage application
- Work closely with presenters to ensure that the program does not become an advertisement for a particular company or agency
- Ask for handouts from presenters in advance for this type of program and have "take away" materials available

Libraries serve as trustworthy institutions within a community, and with some work on your part and the part of the agencies you choose for this program, you can offer a useful and informative program without becoming the mouthpiece for a particular realty agency or lending institution. Buying a home is a huge step for people of any age, but taking this big step might be the cornerstone of feeling "all grown up now" for many younger adults.

CONCLUSION

Programs and services that bring young parents with children, young couples without kids, and young working professionals into the library to share books, programs, discussions or a game night are a big plus for those folks who are finally beginning to settle down. Access to online magazines, movies, audio, and e-books can provide a relaxing evening after a stressful week at work, or a fun family night.

Trusted and established in local communities, libraries are poised to offer services that complement the services offered in daycares and preschools. By engaging with young parents and teaching them how to foster early literacy habits, libraries help to build greater reading skills for children and establish a pattern of life-long learning early on. In addition to improving on the little ones vocabulary and potential reading skills, you are working to create a new generation of library users, while keeping in touch with a generation that often manages to slip away.

CHAPTER 5

Midlife Crisis (or Not): Age Group 40–55

I'm not going to soft-pedal it: This midlife period can be really challenging, or at least it was for me. By now, most of us are pretty firmly entrenched in, if not a particular job, at least a career choice, things start happening with the body that have never happened before, kids are becoming more independent and leaving "the nest" around this time, and some of us get unceremoniously dumped back into the workforce. Then, there is the whole issue of being caught up in the "Sandwich Generation" during this time—dealing with older and ailing parents while trying to raise children of our own. Seriously, it can be rough.

But there really is no such thing as midlife crisis, at least not of the stereotypical "buy a sports car and start having an extramarital affair" variety, or so some people would like us to think (Drimalla, Hanna. "Midlife Myths." *Scientific American Mind* 26.2, pp. 58–61, September 10, 2015). However, midlife brings on a tremendous amount of responsibility and physical changes, and oftentimes with these types of changes comes additional stress. So, while the big, full-blown midlife crisis might be a myth, a series of smaller "challenges" at this time can make a person feel like they are experiencing a real crisis. Been there, done that. By keeping in contact with and offering services and programs of interest to those who so diligently brought their kids in for story hour and early literacy programs just a few years ago, libraries can be a source of help and comfort in a time of real need.

STUCK IN THE MIDDLE

If you are middle-aged, you might fall into the Sandwich Generation category, meaning that you could possibly be caring for an aging parent or relative while taking care of or assisting your own children or even grandchildren. In a 2013 Pew Internet report, "The Sandwich Generation: Rising Financial Burdens for Middle-Aged Americans" (http://www .pewsocialtrends.org/2013/01/30/the-sandwich-generation/), researchers Kim Parker and Eileen Patten reported that nearly 50 percent of all adults in their 40s and 50s had a parent over the age of 65 while raising a younger child or still supporting an older child. Fifteen percent of this age group were contributing to the financial support of both the younger child and the older parent at the same time. While millennials are increasingly taking up some of burden of caregiving in many instances, the older female is still the main caregiver at this point in history. This is not a good time to lose a job or make a risky career change, yet economic factors such as a downturn in the economy can often lead to this very thing.

In an article for the *Wall Street Journal*, William Power, a financial reporter, writes about his personal experience in dealing with his elderly in-laws' financial situation. "The Difficult, Delicate Untangling of our Parents' Financial Lives" describes his experience with his wife in unraveling the mysteries of the financial lives of a couple who was married for over 50 years and found themselves physically and mentally unable to take care of their own finances. In the article, Power concludes with how he and his wife are planning for the time when they will no longer be able to handle their own finances by having

- a clear, comprehensive list of assets,
- a similar list of debts,
- account passwords and usernames for all online accounts, kept in a secure location, and
- a trusted family member who knows the location of all of this information.

Providing a program or link to resources on "Guidance for those Assisting the Elderly with Finances" could be a great benefit to the Sandwich Generation (http://www.wsj.com/articles/the-difficult-delicate -untangling-of-our-parents-financial-lives-1459130770).

The Caregiver Generation

The Sandwich Generation is also most often the Caregiver Generation, and no matter when you were born, every generation goes through a "Sandwich" period in which middle-aged people can be found caring for older adults and their own offspring at the same time. Caregiving for aging parents while taking care of children or assisting young adults can be a time-consuming task, yet many people contribute to the care of another while holding down full-time or part-time jobs. There are a number of useful facts about caregiving in the United States to be found in the executive summary of a study done by the National Alliance for Caregiving in collaboration with AARP. According to the summary, titled "Caregiving in the U.S.":

- The out-of-pocket costs for caregivers average $200–$324 per month.
- Caregivers report having difficulty finding time for friends or family (51%), giving up hobbies or other activities (44%), and having less time for such self-care activities as exercise (26%).
- One third of all caregivers report emotional distress over their situation.
- More than 44 million unpaid caregivers provide care to someone age 18 and older who is ill or has a disability.
- An estimated 16 percent or 33.9 million Americans provide unpaid care to adults over 50.
- The typical caregiver is a 46-year-old woman with some college education, providing more than 20 hours of care each week to her mother.
- About 73 percent of surveyed caregivers said praying helps them cope with caregiving stress, 61 percent said that they talk with or seek advice from friends or relatives, and 44 percent read about caregiving in books or other materials.
- About 30 percent said they need help keeping the person they care for safe and 27 percent would like to find easy activities to do with the person they care for.
- Caregivers need assistance with locating materials in their native language.
- They need more information about the medications their charges take.

This same report states that 60 percent of all caregivers are female, with the greatest number of Hispanics (21.0%), followed by African Americans (20.3%) providing care for someone at home.

More female caregivers felt that they had no choice in deciding to offer care (42%), usually for financial reasons, while only 34 percent of males felt this way (https://assets.aarp.org/rgcenter/il/us_caregiving_1.pdf).

This kind of caregiving frequently takes its toll on the caregiver's own health and well-being and as each Sandwich Generation grows older, new health concerns of their own crop up. Unfortunately for many, it is from the 40s onward that health concerns too often become a major focal point of our lives. Libraries can offer valuable services to those caregivers through assistance with locating local resources, reliable information about medication, and informative and inspirational reading and programming to make this demanding job easier.

LIBRARIES CARING FOR THE CAREGIVERS

There are a number of ways in which libraries can help with caring for the caregiver. In addition to the reliable health resources offered by the National Network of Libraries of Medicine mentioned in Chapter 3, offering additional resources on caregiving for those folks caught between a younger and older generation is a must. The U.S. Department of Health and Senior Service's National Institute on Aging offers caregivers print publications such as booklets on the following:

- Home Safety for People with Alzheimer's Disease
- Hospitalization
- Safe Use of Medicines

And fact sheets on:

- Bathing
- Caring for Yourself
- Changes in Communications Skills
- Coping with Agitation and Aggression
- Disaster Preparedness
- Driving Safety
- Exercise and Physical Activity
- Hallucinations, Delusions, and Paranoia
- Helping Kids Understand Alzheimer's Disease, Home Safety
- Long-Distance Caregiving—Getting Started

While many of these issues are related to Alzheimer's care, another online resource offers more general caregiving information.

The National Caregivers Library at http://www.caregiverslibrary.org/home.aspx offers links to everything from government agencies to resources for working caregivers to end-of-life and legal matters. A link to these online resources on your library's website could provide instant access to a well-compiled listing of agencies, publications, and tools for caregivers.

Housing Resources for Older Parents

When caregiving becomes too much of a responsibility, and it can, there are agencies that can assist caregivers in locating assisted living or other housing for aging parents. Provide links on the library's website to the following:

- Administration for Community Living (www.aoa.gov): The Administration for Community Living (ACL) is part of the U.S. Department of Health and Human Services and is headed by the administrator, who reports directly to the Secretary of Health and Human Services (HHS). ACL serves as the federal agency responsible for providing access to community support and resources for older adults and people with disabilities.
- Eldercare.gov (www.eldercare.gov): A public service of the Administration on Aging, U.S. Department of Health and Human Services, is a nationwide service that connects older Americans and their caregivers with information on senior services, including a searchable database of Area Agencies on Aging, State Units on Aging, aging information and referral programs, Aging and Disability Resources Centers, and special purpose information and assistance resources for legal services, elder abuse prevention, health insurance counseling, and the Long-Term Care Ombudsman Program.
- U.S. Department of Housing and Urban Development (www.hud .gov): U.S. Department of Housing and Urban Development (HUD) offers housing options, including assistance with research to determine the kind of assistance or living arrangement needed, health insurance coverage; and affordability. HUD-approved housing counselors offer further assistance and information about ways to stay in the home, reverse mortgages for seniors, federal housing programs for seniors, rural housing loans, apartment locator, units for the elderly and persons with disabilities and public housing.
- The National Council on Aging (www.ncoa.org): It offers an online search tool for older adults and caregivers, including assistance with Medicare, food assistance programs, and paying for medications.
- Department of Veterans Affairs (www.va.gov): It provides information about benefits, including disability and survivor benefits.

COLLECTION DEVELOPMENT AND PROGRAMS

"Beef up" your career subject areas with titles that are more specific to mid-career adults, or books that specifically address the issues of starting over or changing careers midlife, such as the following:

- *Midlife Career Change in a 20-Something World: How to Find Happiness in a Career Transition after 40* by Sarah Guilliot
- *The Sequel: How to Change Your Career without Starting Over* by Laurence Shatkin
- *Strategize to Win: The New Way to Start Out, Step Up, or Start Over in Your Career* by Carla A. Harris
- *Rebounders: How Winners Pivot from Setback to Success* by Rick Newman
- *Do What You Are: Discover the Perfect Career* by Paul D. Tieger, Barbara Barron, and Kelly Tieger

Focus more on books that would help a user finally find his or her niche in life, like the ever-popular and ever-updated *What Color Is Your Parachute?* by Richard N. Bolles and *The Pathfinder: How to Choose or Change Your Career for a Lifetime of Satisfaction and Success* by Nicholas Lore. It is probably a safe bet that many people changing careers will want to read and research before taking the plunge into a new career, so having fresh titles on hand either in print or e-book format will be a benefit for this demographic.

Two very obvious career choices for those changing careers in midlife are

1. teacher and
2. consultant

I say obvious because having gained the kind of experience that folks in mid-career have often obtained, making a career out of offering that expertise that comes with experience to others is a good fit. Preparing for the Praxis exam can be done through Learning Express Library, as well as preparation for civil service exams, resume building, and ways to improve job searching, networking, and interview skills.

Programming for Empty Nesters: Is Our House Getting Bigger or What?

Some middle-aged folks find themselves in a completely different situation from the Caregivers—these are the Empty Nesters. Now that all of the little nestlings have flown away to college or career, mom and dad are still doing well enough in a senior living community, and suddenly, the house seems too big and too empty. Such a big change in the life force field could produce all kinds of results—the need for a new career, a new hobby, new home decorating, downsizing to smaller place, or the urge to get out of stale relationships, whether with a partner or a career. Something has got to change!

You can almost think of the empty nesters as starting over again but hopefully without the financial insecurity and lack of experience of 20 years ago. Empty nesters need something to do, and their interests have probably changed over the years or at least their approach to the same interest might be different: the young man who started a garage band could still be interested in music, just maybe not banging on drums in the basement any more. The woman who participated in teen summer reading many years ago could once again have time for an Adult Summer Reading (ASR) program or adult book club. The crafter, writer, painter, composer, and DIYer just maybe wants to be able to do some of those things once again.

Just as story hour was important to the preschooler and the parents of the preschooler, programming can become increasingly important as kids leave the nest and parents have a bit more "free time" on their hands. These newly freed parents might suffer a few pangs of longing for their children, and an Empty Nest support group meeting in the library could be just thing they are looking for. Others might choose to pursue new interests, including a new love life, and some of the kinds of programming mentioned back in Chapter 2 would be in order, such as the following:

- Real estate—tips and tricks for downsizing
- Finances—making the most of savings and investing
- Time management—simple steps to freeing up more time for play
- Home improvement—learn how to do simple home repairs
- Purchasing power—getting the best deals all the time
- Take charge of your health now, reap benefits later—give users a taste of yoga, meditation, or an exercise class
- Budgeting for life expenses
- Home decorating and design
- Computer classes
- Crafting
- Gourmet cooking (by now they have mastered everyday cooking)
- Wine tasting
- Speed dating for divorcees (still based on literary tastes)

By modifying a few programming ideas for a slightly different age group, you can have a handful or a series of programs tailored to the Empty Nesters among your library users.

Midlife Career Changes

Sometimes in midlife, people decide, "To heck with this! I'm going to do what I want to do!" According to a 2014 Gallup Poll, about 30 percent of baby boomers and GenXers are disengaged in their current job positions (http://www.gallup.com/poll/181289/majority-employees-not-engaged-despite-gains-2014.aspx), and it is those 30 percent who could be looking to jump ship at this point in their careers, out of simple boredom or a sense of lack of fulfillment or job satisfaction.

On the other hand, middle-aged workers, often the higher paid employees after having gained knowledge and experience in their field, can be the first ones to be unceremoniously dumped when there is an economic downturn or company merger. A midlife career change can also feel like a midlife crisis, unless the career changer has instigated the change of his or her own will! And a midlife career change is just a bit more serious than your average job hopping early in one's career. This type of move takes some soul searching and a feeling of confidence in what one is about to do.

In *The Mature Mind: The Positive Power of the Aging Brain*, Dr. Gene D. Cohen suggests that the first phase in the aging adult mind is the reevaluation phase, a time in which we start to wonder how many years we really have left. Such reevaluation is often the springboard for a new career, hobby, or a more serious pursuit of a new passion. Offering collections and programs in these areas will benefit your midlife library users.

There Has to Be Something More to Life!

For some, simply changing jobs would not be enough. The urge to finally do what they have always wanted to do could cause these midlife career jumpers to take the plunge and start a new business. Programming and classes will be beneficial to this group, as starting a new business requires knowledge of business markets in specific areas, and networking. This type of information is best found in immediate and frequently updated sources, and not so much in a print resource. Consider hosting programs that feature like-minded individuals who have already started a new business, current business owners, and organizations devoted to local businesses, like the local area Chamber of Commerce or other economic development organizations.

Key to establishing a new business with sustained growth, particularly for older, career-minded library users, is having the right resources available and the knowledge to use them effectively. While many very serious younger entrepreneurs will take on the challenge of starting a new business, there can be much more at stake for those switching careers at midlife. The library can offer additional programming and marketing of resources already in place as well as new offerings in the area of business resources. A well-trained library staff can assist library users with finding industry facts, consumer trends, and other valuable business information, and provide community connections with prospects and colleagues through monthly networking events and trainings. Library users looking for consultation about business plans, use of computers and computer software and training with specific business-related software, will benefit from classroom and training provided by knowledgeable library staff.

In order to better serve the business community, aspiring entrepreneurs, and job seekers, the library should invest in providing access and assistance with at least some of the following online and print resources:

- A collection of print and electronic business books, on topics such as decision making, globalization, project management, negotiation, and leadership
- EBSCO's Business Source Complete database
- Business Insights Essentials database
- Morningstar Investment Research Center online
- Small Business Resource Center online
- Online journals
- Business Plan Pro, a software program designed for creating business plans

Job seeking and career development

- Gale Vocations and Careers Collection
- Gale Testing and Education Reference Center database
- Cypress Resume Builder

Grant research and writing

- Foundation Center Philanthropy In/Sight
- Foundation Directory Online
- Foundation Grants to Individuals Online

Business and financial news

- Online databases such as Standard & Poor's
- Print business newspapers and investor newsletters
- Weekly print publication Value Line, covering 3,500 stocks and 1,900 mutual funds on a quarterly basis

Services

- Appointments for a personal consultation with a librarian to discuss resources designed to assist with business, career, or financial concerns
- Free classes, such as résumé creation, Internet and software basics, and job search strategies, and a monthly networking opportunity, possibly in partnership with the Chamber of Commerce or local economic development organizations

The success of any library program relies heavily upon outreach and marketing. Without proper marketing, library collections and services, while excellent resources, often remain underused due to lack of exposure to the community at large. By marketing services to local businesses and entrepreneurs, the library will quickly become a recognized and contributing factor in the business community.

Consider offering the following:

- Monthly after-work "happy hours" for networking opportunities, finding potential customers, and making new connections
- Classroom instruction that will provide the means of not only learning a new searching skill or software but also an opportunity to meet like-minded people with similar business goals and interests
- User-based skill training software for customers, such as Lynda.com
- Book discussions led by local business leaders on hot topics in the industry
- A session on federal government contracts
- A session on the Patent and Trademark Repositories of the United State Patent and Trademark Office (USPTO) and their resources
- Introduction to any of the business-related online databases or software currently in place; rotate these offerings on a weekly basis and at varying times to accommodate schedules
- Resume building techniques using online and in-house library resources

- Coordination of business mentorships with members from the Service Corp of Retired Executives business counselors and interested individuals
- A discussion on small business loans from local bankers or representatives of the U.S. Small Business Administration
- A tutorial in LinkedIn for business
- A presentation on how to write a business plan
- An introduction to social media for business

Outreach and Marketing

Promoting the library's services and programs will require a variety of outreach and marketing techniques, including

- the attention of local news outlets via ads, press releases, and articles
- presentations to local service and business support organizations
- mailings to local businesses
- simple word-of-mouth

MORE DETAILED PROGRAMMING IDEAS

Local Business Owners' Fair

For those people experiencing their own "Is this all there is in life?" moment, or those who have been unceremoniously dumped out of their jobs of several years, the midlife crisis is real, folks. If you suddenly notice an influx of people who should be at work during the day, it is time to offer some midlife career-changing programs. Realizing that the entrepreneurial spirit is still alive and well in many middle-aged people, some programming to spark that spirit is in order.

Learning goals:

- Learn about successful local businesses
- Have an opportunity to converse with local business owners
- Learn some keys to success
- Connect with like-minded individuals and network
- Learn about business related library resources

Steps to take:

- Find local business owners who would like to share their success stories with others

- Have a space large enough to accommodate some displays as well as seating and presenters
- Take applications for the business fair, as there will probably be quite a bit of interest
- Have a series of short presentations by different business owners over the course of the day, allowing attendees to come and go, as desired
- Allow people to toot their own horns
- Allow business owners to set up and leave displays for browsing
- Make sure that presenters know they are sharing the story of how they began and the "secrets to success"
- Have a display of business related and entrepreneurial book selections around the library
- Do your own presentation on online and print business resources, emphasizing the ways in which the library can help
- Provide links to local and federal e-government resources for small businesses on the library website
- Follow up with the business owners with written thanks and acknowledgment through the library's website and newsletters as this work will be done "pro bono"

In addition to job searching, resume building, and other standard offerings for career building, a successful local business fair could be a fun and exciting addition to your roster of programs!

Adult Summer Reading Book Club

When I served as Adult Services Consultant for the Missouri State Library, I hosted ASR workshops all around the state. ASR was just taking off at that point, and there was quite a bit of enthusiasm for it. Busy midlifers might enjoy an "excuse" to sit down and read for pleasure once a day. "Hey, I joined this ASR program, I have to finish my reading this week. Laundry will just have to wait!" There are so many wonderful ASR programming ideas to choose from, and the Collaborative Summer Library Program (CSLP), a consortium of states working together to provide high-quality summer reading program materials for children, teens, *and adults*, offers up a different theme each year as well as materials for purchase, and ideas for sharing. The 2017 theme, "build a better world," offers up numerous opportunities for programming. Here is one idea:

Learning goals:

- Learn about different cultures and people in a relaxed and engaging atmosphere

- Highlight a few authors from around the world
- Open up opportunities for discussion on the various refugee crises and the role of other nations in assisting
- Learn about other customs, religions, and traditions
- Find common ground for all people

Steps to take:

- Require online or onsite registration for full participation, such as drawings for prizes and submitting book suggestions for other readers
- Choose a variety of books in different formats to feature through the library website and in displays
- Choose three or four books for group discussion in the old-fashioned onsite book club manner, and allow for postings and discussion online, where possible
- Use any adult committee members that you might have to come up with book ideas for discussion
- Try to find at least one author that can do a presentation with a global theme and failing an onsite presentation, try to do something by Skype
- Video presentations can be kept online long after the actual event, with the presenter's permission
- Check local calendars for conflicts of scheduling for busy adults
- Choose fiction to keep things on the lighter side of discussion and offer carefully balanced political views if venturing into nonfiction
- Invite members of the community representative of readings to add richness and authenticity to discussions
- Have a fun "taste of" whatever country or culture that might be on the list of possibilities, involving community members
- Do a book to movie night for adults and then discuss which is better (ha!)
- If you track the number of books read, try to get some really good prizes such as a night at a local B&B or dinner out for your adults, through donation, if it is not in the library's budget

Make ASR fun and meaningful for your busy midlifers, and they will thank you for it. Everybody needs a reading break now and then.

CONCLUSION

Midlife career changers frequently feel the pressure of caring for younger and older family members, the urge to finally do "the thing" that they have always wanted to do, or face the challenge of being dumped back into the workforce at a time when they least expected it. When offering a comprehensive and dynamic library service to would-be business owners and midlife career changers, ensuring recognition of the service through marketing and outreach is a vital part of the equation and should never be ignored. If they do not know you have it, they cannot use it!

CHAPTER 6

An End in Sight (or Not): Age Group 55–65

It was bound to come to our attention, sooner or later: "Ack! I'm going to be retiring in the next ten years or so!" Thinking about retirement can make us feel really old and creaky, really, really, happy, or somewhere in between. Thinking about retirement either fills us with fear and anxiety or causes us to spin off into some quiet little daydream about all those things we will finally be able to do. I personally fall into the latter category. Whatever the case may be, considering retirement does cause us to face some issues that we might have swept under the carpet for a couple of decades, such as the following:

1. Am I financially able to actually retire?
2. Do I have enough in savings?
3. What should I do about my investments?
4. What about insurance after retirement?
5. Most importantly, which senior discounts kick in before age 65?

While I do not personally have the answer to any of these questions, I know that I can find the answers if I do my research or get in contact with people who have the expertise that I need. Dealing with such weighty matters definitely calls for some expertise and few of us can afford a $1,000+-an-hour private consultation with a financial planner. At this age, a person also might seriously consider finally writing up a will, or be considering a planned giving option. Practical programs, as well as "flights of fancy," are in order as people begin to see light at the end of the long work tunnel.

In Phase II of the older adult life, as described in *The Mature Mind: The Positive Power of the Aging Brain* (Cohen, 2006), Dr. Cohen refers to "the liberation phase," the point in life where we begin to think more about what we might have missed—the big trip we always planned to take and the social cause we always wanted to stand up for or take part in—and this type of reflection often leads to action. The feeling of "It's now or never" begins to creep into our minds when it comes to thinking about all of the things we might have done.

Coming up with programs and rounding out collections to fill the financial planning gap, spur the imagination, and allow this age group to continue to follow their dreams into retirement are among the services libraries can provide.

LIBRARY SERVICES FOR THE SOON-TO-BE RETIRED

As with any other demographic, people looking toward retirement, but not there yet, generally have different information needs and interests. Financial planning for retirement is most often first and foremost, but other life's issues start to bubble to the surface, too. The idea of doing certain things while we still have the income might be in the minds of some, like travel, looking into the best places to retire in the United States and other countries, and thinking about taking a chance on that "thing" you always thought you should do or be but never found the right time or place to do it or be it. Consider offering programs and emphasizing or expanding collections for the soon-to-be-retiree.

The Circle of Life

Many people at this stage in life find themselves enjoying time with the grandkids. Some people find themselves raising grandchildren, because of family tragedy or other reasons. Whatever the case may be, interacting with younger children at this time can be even more rich and rewarding than the first time around. Many of the same programs and services to younger parents described in Chapter 4 can be applicable to grandparents, whether they are the full-time guardians or weekend caregivers. While one situation might present many more challenges than the other, libraries can and do offer the types of programs that grandparent and child can enjoy together, such as story times, crafting, and game nights.

Many grandparents have the unique opportunity to share more quality time with grandchildren than they might have shared with their own children, due to work requirements or the hectic scheduling of caring for multiple children at once. Educating grandparents with some of the same reading and discussion techniques found in programs like "Every Child Ready to

Read" and "Prime Time Family Reading Time" could just be invaluable to the child's development, depending on family circumstances, and if nothing else, aid in bonding between grandparent and grandchild.

Also, just as in Chapter 4, as there are those who might only have fur babies, or have a combination of children and fur babies, there are older adults who might even get to enjoy their adult children's "grandpets." I know this, as I have a friend who speaks of keeping the "grandcats." While programming with grandpets in mind might be difficult to plan (for how often might a group of people be called upon to cat sit at one time?), having a display of relevant books and other materials on caring for pets for those without pets could be a good idea. Pet sitting, dog walking, and caring for pets while their owners are away can also be a form of extra income, so programming around pet sitting and dog walking could be of interest to several age groups. Responsible adults are called upon to do all sorts of things in life. Do not limit your imagination when it comes to book displays, programs, and collection development!

Planning for a New Life: It Is Never Too Soon to Dream

While people in the 55–65-year-old age group do have the responsibility to be financially prepared for their retirement, it is not too early to start planning for what we will do with all that spare time! In a survey by American Association of Retired Persons (AARP) of nearly 5,000 workers ages 50 to 64, more than one-third of those polled expect to continue to work, preferably part-time, after retirement and a full 44 percent of that group would like to work in a different field from their current job (http://blog.aarp.org/2015/09/08/aarp-survey-todays-retirement-dream -often-includes-a-job/). I know there are some who say, "What would I do with myself if I retired?" There are others of us who have one eye on the nearest exit, with a concrete plan for what we will do when we finally do not have to get up, shower, and face rush hour traffic. This is the fun kind of retirement planning!

Treating this type of "exploratory" retirement planning somewhat like planning for a second career might be one way to approach it for those clueless about what they might like to do, with a focus on interests and compatibility in certain areas. We all know someone who has made their living in one field, while keeping an avid interest in and connection to another field, and those who dabble in many things in their spare time. For example, I have made my living working in libraries and archives, but I originally studied music as an undergraduate and graduate student and would love to be able to teach voice when I have the supplemental income and freedom that retirement will one day bring. Being able to finally devote full attention to an avocation could be a lovely thing indeed.

COLLECTION DEVELOPMENT AND PROGRAMS

For this type of programming and collection development, give your library users an opportunity to delve into their personal interests and hobbies in depth through collections and offer programming that relates to career aptitude and personality type. Who knows? The lifetime hobby could end up being a second career or lucrative part-time job in retirement, fostered by a little self-curiosity, some planning, and research. Look to add or emphasize existing resources on self-employment, career-related personality and aptitude, and skills transfer.

One obvious choice for nonfiction reading at this stage is retirement planning. Try to include titles that address the various aspects of planning for retirement, not just financial planning, including plans for continued work in retirement or being free to pursue old or new dreams and goals.

- *The New Rules of Retirement: Strategies for a Secure Future* by Robert C. Carlson
- *The 5 Years before You Retire: Retirement Planning When You Need It the Most* by Emily Guy Birken
- *How to Retire Happy: The 12 Most Important Decisions You Must Make before You Retire,* Fourth Edition, by Stan Hinden
- *Retire Inspired: It's Not an Age, It's a Financial Number* by Chris Hogan
- *Too Young to Retire: 101 Ways to Start the Rest of Your Life* by Marika Stone
- *Portfolio Life: The New Path to Work, Purpose, and Passion after 50* by David D. Corbett
- *Make Your Own Living Trust* by Denis Clifford, Attorney
- *Your Estate Matters: Gifts, Estates, Wills, Trusts, Taxes and Other Estate Planning Issues* by Patti S. Spencer
- *Pet Sitting: End Money Worries Business Book: Pet Sitters Secrets to Starting, Financing, Marketing and Making Massive Money* by Brian Mahoney
- *How to Build a Pet Sitting and Boarding Business (Special Edition): The Only Book You Need to Launch, Grow & Succeed* by T. K. Johnson

More mature readers still like to read for entertainment and will no doubt continue to read in their favorite genres, but reading to learn something new is also an attractive proposition. Be sure to include new biographies and books on current events in your collection for older readers.

The Not-So-Golden Parachute

- Since statistics show that many of the average working types (like me) do not have enough in savings or in a pension plan, and the "Golden Parachute" fails to open for most of us, we might be looking for a different kind (or color) of retirement parachute. According to a 2016 Gallup Poll report, "Three in 10 U.S. Workers Foresee Working Past Retirement Age" by Lydia Saad, 31 percent of workers plan to work beyond the age of 67. Also found in this report:
  - A quarter of seniors are currently working beyond retirement age.
  - 23 percent expect to retire before the age of 62.
  - And the largest percentage, 38 percent, will retire somewhere between the ages of 62 and 67. (http://www.gallup.com/poll/ 191477/three-workers-foresee-working-past-retirement-age.aspx)

Programming based on the *What Color Is Your Parachute?* series or something similar can assist career changers or retirement planners in honing in on what they might be ideally suited to do, if they have not found their niche yet. Having some additional income during retirement could be a necessity for many of us. Again, try to make use of online career aptitude or personality quizzes to assist library users in finding their niche and then further their quest for what to do next by highlighting print and electronic resources found in the library and online. Career aptitude tools can be found at by searching the following:

- The AARP Foundation's Work and Jobs Site online
- AARP Back to Work 50+ online
- The Career Interest Game, University of Missouri online
- Meyers-Briggs personality tests online

Getting the Financial Ducks in a Row

The U.S. Department of Labor (USDOL) shares these statistics in *Top 10 Ways to Prepare for Retirement*:

- Fewer than half of Americans have calculated how much they need to save for retirement

- In 2012, 30 percent of private industry workers with access to a defined contribution plan (such as a 401(k) plan) did not participate
- The average American spends 20 years in retirement

The National Institute on Retirement Security (NIRS) in a 2013 report also paints a pretty grim picture about retirement savings:

> The average working household has virtually no retirement savings. When all households are included—not just households with retirement accounts—the median retirement account balance is $3,000 for all working-age households and $12,000 for near-retirement households. Two-thirds of working households age 55–64 with at least one earner have retirement savings less than one times their annual income, which is far below what they will need to maintain their standard of living in retirement. (http://www.nirsonline.org/storage/nirs/documents/Retirement%20Savings%20Crisis/retirementsavingscrisis_final.pdf)

The USDOL offers a number of pamphlets, fact sheets, and even an interactive worksheet that allows one to calculate monthly income and expenses in retirement (http://askebsa.dol.gov/retirementcalculator/ui/general.aspx). Another retirement calculator can be found on the Social Security Administration's website. These calculators are a particularly useful tool, and while it is a little scary to actually see what your monthly retirement benefit will be, the calculator provides an honest assessment, which will allow a person to play "catch up" with retirement savings in those final years before retiring. NIRS also offers a Pension Education Toolkit, which addresses cost of living adjustments, with a Cost of Living Adjustment calculator, and state-by-state facts and figures, including the types of retirement benefits offered by state governments and teacher retirement systems. While librarians are not financial advisors, we can become familiar enough with online tools and resources to offer an overview of the same to our library users. Preparing your own programs or finding local financial advisors to provide programming can be a great benefit to current and would-be library users at this stage in life.

Programs with Saving Money in Mind

Plan programs using overarching umbrella themes for several months or a year. Having umbrella themes was a good tool for program planning. Choosing an umbrella theme for an entire year allows a program planner to focus on more specific goals and create better outcomes, rather than looking at programming as a grab bag of ideas. One of those themes that you might use for this user group is financial planning or ways in which to save money. Here are a couple of suggestions for money saving programs.

Living off the Grid—Eco-Living

A program on living "off grid" or eco-living could be a good choice for the current wave of soon-to-be retirees. After all, the pre and newly retired at this time are children of the 1960s and 1970s, a time when young people in America really became interested in the environment, in eco-farming and the effects of pesticides and pollutants on the food we eats. Many of those same young people grew up to be the green grocers and eco-farmers as adults, and they may not have been able to accomplish all of their eco-minded goals in life. Living off grid is not only good for the environment, but good for the wallet, once the initial costs of going off grid have been expended. In the course of a program about eco-friendly living, participants could

1. find out about the basic living off the grid concepts,
2. discover how to start living off the grid the ideal way (solar power, etc.), and
3. learn realistic ways to reduce reliance on the grid.

Consider the following as guests for the presentation:

* A live-off-the-grid guru with tips on how to save money through innovative living, perhaps even be a local architect who is involved in Leadership in Energy and Environmental Design (LEED)
* Local organic urban farmer or representative from a community supported agriculture (CSA), local county extension personnel who could discuss growing and canning vegetables, or raising chickens
* Solar power installer who can demonstrate and answer questions about the up-front costs of solar power, and the financial and environmental benefits in the long term

The perfect timing for this type of program is mid-to-late April, coinciding with Earth Day, each April 22.

As with all programs, be sure to tie into library resources, such as the most energy efficient appliances to be found in *Consumer Reports*, or books and digital resources available, such as the following:

- *Living Off the Grid: Off-Grid Living and Starting a Homestead from Scratch—Amazing DIY Projects for Self Sufficient Living!* by Isaac Green
- *DIY Projects for the Self-Sufficient Homeowner: 25 Ways to Build a Self-Reliant Lifestyle* by Betsy Matheson
- *The Moneyless Man: A Year of Freeconomic Living* by Mark Boyle
- *Thriving during Challenging Times: The Energy, Food, and Financial Independence Handbook* by Cam Mather
- *Off on Our Own: Living Off-Grid in Comfortable Independence* by Ted Carns

Second Careers

As one of those who look forward to doing what I had always hoped to do in life, it was always difficult to understand those who would wring their hands and say, "I just don't know what I will do when I retire." In the years preceding retirement, many people will start to look forward to the day when they can finally paint, or teach music, write the great American novel, or even take up a second career in the business world. Offering a program that will assist those anticipating a second career after retirement is a great idea. Learning goals for such a program would be as follows:

1. Learn how to create an up to date résumé (especially digital)
2. Discover local resources for finding jobs (job services, state agencies)
3. Learn how to use technology based networking platforms to find jobs (Monster, Indeed, LinkedIn)
4. Create a resume based on volunteer or avocational activities
5. Learn to market skills that might have been "dormant" for some time through a life coach or career counselor

Potential guests:

- A local job service office representative, career counselor, or life coach
- An HR or hiring officer to talk about what they look for in potential new hires
- Student volunteers to help with digital resume creation

Suggested Books for the Library Collection

The Encore Career Handbook: How to Make a Living and a Difference in the Second Half of Life by Marci Alboher

Second-Act Careers: 50+ Ways to Profit from Your Passions during Semi-Retirement by Nancy Collamer

Too Young to Retire: 101 Ways to Start the Rest of Your Life by Marika Stone

Portfolio Life: The New Path to Work, Purpose, and Passion after 50 by David D. Corbett

Unique Adult Career Guide 2017 Edition: Offering Career Advice and Listing 100 Different Careers by Dawn Lucan

Selling Online: A Second "Job"

In addition to those who might be thinking of taking on a new job in retirement, or finally getting to do what they have always wanted to do, there are entrepreneurial spirits out there who make a living or supplement their income through online sales. The Internet is the biggest marketplace of all, and if a person is willing to put in the work, the rewards can be worth it.

Such a program would consist of presenters who are knowledgeable about websites such as eBay, where a person can buy anything from a car to ramen noodles, Etsy, which is devoted to arts and crafts, and Craigslist, which allows users to advertise and "shop locally" for just about anything, from real estate to companionship. A panel consisting of collectors, antiquers, and bargain shoppers would also be useful in rounding out this program. Knowing how to "buy low" and "sell high" is a skill that many lack. Tie into the library's collections with some books, such as the following:

My eBay for Seniors by Michael Miller

The Everything Guide to Selling Arts & Crafts Online: How to Sell on Etsy, eBay, Your Storefront, and Everywhere Else Online by Kim Solga

Start a Business: How to Work from Home Making Money Selling on eBay by T. Whitmore

The Complete Idiot's Guide to Making Money with Craigslist by Skip Press

eBay Photos That Sell: Taking Great Product Shots for eBay and Beyond by Dan Gookin and Robert Birnbach

The Handmade Marketplace: How to Sell Your Crafts Locally, Globally, and On-Line by Kari Chapin

How to Make Money Using Etsy: A Guide to the Online Marketplace for Crafts and Handmade Products by Timothy Adam

Living the Dream: Is It Now or Never?

While some seniors are able to afford travel in retirement, many of us figure that we would better try to squeeze in any big travel while we still have a steady income and good knees! Younger people frequently do not have the leisure time or financial resources, or have small children and other obligations that hamper extensive traveling. In those years leading up to retirement, when the nest is empty and some financial stability has been achieved, an "It's now or never" attitude about finally seeing Michelangelo's David or Machu Picchu can creep in. A study by the Transamerica Center for Retirement found that travel is one of the top two goals for retirement, yet only one in five Americans has factored savings into their retirement plan (http://www.transamericacenter.org/docs/default-source/resources/travel-survey/tcrs2013_sr_travel_and_aging.pdf). So, maybe for some of us, it really is now or never!

Travel programs designed for this specific age group can provide a more relaxed atmosphere for those looking forward to retirement, while trying to squeeze in some travel time now. Be sure to include some financial programs on saving for travel in retirement. A quick and easy program is to engage experienced travelers to share their own experiences and provide an overview of online resources and tools for finding travel deals or travel inspiration, such as

- TravelZoo
- TravelMuse
- TripAdvisor
- TravelChannel.com/Destinations

Or start an "It's Now or Never" travel group for those 50+. Programming can be a part of the group, but just allowing them a place to meet and share travel ideas or discuss travel deals can be a good start. Use travel themed books, book discussions, and programs based on different culture's foods and music to provide a taste of some exotic locale for your travel-related programming. Inspiring people to learn about different culture, and, in turn, to maybe explore these cultures through travel, can be a good fit for the "It's Now or Never" group. Also focusing on specialized vacations, such as cuisines, cycling or sports, or hobby-related activities, are a good way to create interesting travel programs for this age group. Always tie any programming into the library collections and other events and activities in the community, when possible. In addition to Fodors, Frommers, National Geographic, and Rick Steve's travel guides, look for less well-known, or specialized travel guides for this type of programming, such as the following:

Lonely Planet's Ultimate Travel: Our List of the 500 Best Places to See by Lonely Planet

1,000 Places to See Before You Die: Revised Second Edition by Patricia Schultz

Atlas Obscura: An Explorer's Guide to the World's Hidden Wonders by Joshua Foer and Dylan Thuras

Frommer's Easy Guide to River Cruising by Fran Golden and Michelle Baran

The Cyclist's Bucket List: A Celebration of 75 Quintessential Cycling by Ian Dille

Bucket List Adventures: 10 Incredible Journeys to Experience before You Die by Annette White

My Travel Adventures and Secret Recipes: Culinary Adventures with Secret Recipes by Chef Wolfgang Hanau

1,000 Foods to Eat before You Die: A Food Lover's Life List by Mimi Sheraton

Preretirement-age folk with an adventurous outlook on life and bucket list of goals for travel might enjoy this "it's now or never" type of programming.

The Ultimate in Travel: Dual Residency or Self-Expatriation

Many retirees are taking advantage of better and cheaper health care, sunny climates, and the bang for their American buck that moving to another country can bring them in retirement, but this sort of thing takes some careful planning, which should ideally take place *before* your last day on the job! While it might not be possible to find someone who has actually retired to another country for your presentation, some study of resources available through the AARP could offer enough material to "create your own" program. An AARP article by Barry Golson (*AARP The Magazine*, September/October 2012 issue) lists 10 of the best places to retire abroad. *Best Places to Retire Abroad: Paradise Found 10 Fun,*

Affordable and Stunningly Beautiful Places to Retire Abroad suggests Argentina, Costa Rica, Italy, France, Portugal, and Spain, among other destinations, as good locations for retirement. On the AARP website, you will also find a list of questions to ask before making the move, and more terrifically an Expat Starter Kit. Using these tools, anyone could create their own program, if finding someone who has done the research or perhaps already has dual citizenship in another country. This could make for a very exciting and different kind of "planning for retirement" program (http://www.aarp.org/home-garden/livable-communities/info-07 -2010/paradise_found.html).

Since such a move would require considerable planning, make sure that the library has newer resources on hand, such as the following:

> *The ABA Consumer Guide to Retiring Abroad: Legal, Financial, and Tax Issues and Solutions* by George Hayduk
>
> *The Financial Guide to Retiring Abroad: How to Live Overseas and Avoid Tax, Invest Wisely, and Save Your Money* by Rick Todd
>
> *The International Living Guide to Retiring Overseas on a Budget: How to Live Well on $25,000 a Year* by Suzan Haskins and Dan Prescher
>
> *Best Places to Retire: The Top 15 Affordable Towns for Retirement in Europe* by Clayton Geoffreys
>
> *The Happy Expat: Your Guide to Joyfully Retiring Abroad* by Ann Hoffman

MORE DETAILED PROGRAMMING IDEAS

Financial Preparation for Retirement

Facing retirement in the next decade or so, the reality of no longer having a day-to-day job with a steady income hits home for many, and planning for retirement takes up more and more of a person's time and energy. Assisting older adults with retirement planning before it is too late provides a beneficial service to this demographic. This programming idea probably calls for a series, or at the very least a lengthy workshop. Planning for retirement is multipronged and over simplification can lead to problems down the road.

Learning goals:

- Learn how to calculate how much is "enough" in retirement
- Learn how to invest savings for maximum benefit
- Learn about insurance options in retirement

Steps to take:

- Engage a financial planning expert to present at least two programs on the subject
- Budget for honorarium or speaker's fees
- Advertise through social media, as well as more traditional

Now or Never Vacation Destinations

Not everyone will be able to travel in retirement. Some of us would not be able to afford it, others will have knees that give out, and still others will just be too tired. Offer a program in which a travel agent or an individual who arranges private tours can speak about and arrange trips, according to the groups taste and budget. This seems especially good for older men and women who are widowed or divorced and really do not like the thought of traveling alone. By allowing singles to share a room, they can beat the single room supplement problem. A travel program for those planning for retirement or those already retired with substantial income and knee cartilage can be a beneficial and popular program for the "it's now or never" traveler.

- Learn about travel destinations
- Share travel stories
- Learn about the pros and cons of group travel
- Choose locations for group travel plans
- Meet fellow travel hounds
- Learn about the library's travel resources

Steps to take:
Find local organizations, individuals, or travel agents who provide travel advice or arrangement

- Plan a single program to gauge interest
- Gauge interest in forming a recurring group by surveying attendees at program
- Advertise through Facebook, the library's website, and traditional newsletter or e-mail lists
- Set up the space for showing photos or video
- Provide a variety of travel guides, such as Frommer's, Fodor's, and Lonely Planet, and travel magazines to generate ideas and discussion
- Add links to the library website for travel websites such as AARP, Trip Advisor, or TravelMuse

- Unless you plan to travel with the group, stay out of the arrangements and planning
- Allow the group to grow and change organically as people come and go, join and drop out

Traveling in a group can give a greater sense of safety and offer a boost of courage for timid travelers. For others, just the opportunity to share travel experiences could be the reward. Let the minds and bodies of your older library users roam the earth at will.

CONCLUSION

The preretirement years call for some looking into the future and planning accordingly, even when we may not want to. By using online tools to create programs on retirement planning, assessing aptitudes and interests for exploring new careers, travel, or any other ideas you and these library users might come up with, you can hone your relationship with a demographic that is likely to be more financially secure and interested in exploring new avenues at this stage in life.

CHAPTER 7

Now I Can Finally Relax (or Not): Age Group 65–75

According to *The Baby Boom Cohort in the United States: 2012 to 2060* by Sandra L. Colby and Jennifer M. Ortman, published by the U.S. Census Bureau, "The baby boomers began turning 65 in 2011 and are now driving growth at the older ages of the population. By 2029, when all of the baby boomers will be 65 years and over, more than 20 percent of the total U.S. population will be over the age of 65. Although the number of baby boomers will decline through mortality, this shift toward an increasingly older population is expected to endure. By 2056, the population 65 years and over is projected to become larger than the population under 18 years" (https://www.census.gov/prod/2014pubs/p25-1141.pdf). Therefore, one should not expect library services to seniors to become less critical or needful in at least the next three to four decades. The baby boom wave of retirees has only just begun, and baby boomers will put their unique stamp on the face of retirement in much the same way that they have throughout the course of their lives.

JUMPING INTO RETIREMENT OR NOT?

Current marketing toward older adults includes images depicting fit, gray-haired men and women engaging in all sorts of activities—lounging on a beach in a soaking tub, playing golf, cruising, sailing, jazzercising, hiking, and skydiving—and these images suggest that the baby boom generation must be literally jumping into retirement. Certainly, we are fighting the image of aging more than past generations, or at least advertisers want us to believe that to be true.

While some of the images of the wining, dining, dancing, and skydiving grandma ring true for the boomer generation, there is also much, much evidence that many baby boomers cannot afford to retire, while others are forced to retire due to health concerns, family obligations, or even age discrimination, and suffer financially for it. According to a blog by Buck Wango at the Huffington Post, "Baby Boomers Can't Quit: Still Want to Work after They 'Retire,' " many boomers, even though they are officially "retired," do not necessarily stop working or even want to have retired in the first place. Wango reports from a study from Banker's Life Center for a Secure Retirement "that even though 72 percent of retired Baby Boomers aren't working for pay, there's a large group that is," and almost half of this group would like to work but are unable to due to health issues, caregiving duties, or because they cannot find a job. This study also shows that the majority of retired boomers would have liked to have continued to work but were forced to retire out of circumstances beyond their control, such as health and caregiving issues mentioned earlier.

Among retired boomers, about one-third of them are working because they want to. Conversely, of those not yet retired, almost two-thirds are working because they have to. The article suggests that retirement does not necessarily mean not working at all but "no longer doing your primary career." While money is the top reason for continuing to work after retirement from a primary career, many retirees work for other reasons, such as the mental and physical challenge, social interaction, and greater sense of purpose. Even if the baby boomers were the generation to "shake things up" and "do their own thing," economic and physical changes obviously affect whether or not they are able to retire (http://www .huffingtonpost.com/buck-wargo/baby-boomers-cant-quit-st_b_7621540 .html).

Libraries are in a unique position to not only serve this demographic but also to reap the benefits of insuring a continuing relationship with new full-time and part-time retirees. Having grown up and used libraries all their lives, retirees from the baby boom generation are looking for volunteer opportunities, a cause to support, and a chance to still contribute to society. The local public library can provide an array of services, programs, volunteer, and giving opportunities for these movers and shakers.

LIBRARY SERVICES TO ACTIVE SENIORS

So now that we have established that newly retired baby boomers are not acting like the retirees of previous generations, you might want to give some thought to how you relate to them. Whatever level of service you can afford or choose to offer, try to be creative with the name you give the service or program. Using the term "senior" with baby boomers just does not have the caché that you might need to build around this new or expanded service. How about something like the following:

- Wisdom in Aging Project
- Chapter II Project
- Second Act Library Services
- Late Bloomers Club
- Next Phase Finders Group

Whatever you call your service to this demographic, really promote what you are doing as a special service to them. Let them know that you will give them advanced notice of programs that they might like to see or classes or book discussions to take part in. A very simple service would be to create and add to an e-mail list after every program geared toward older adults, and use it as a means of promoting future programs or communicating additions to your collections. I am promoting an e-mail list, because e-mail is like the new "old snail mail" to me. People of my generation still like to get an e-mail, while younger people only want a text message and heaven forbid that one should place a phone call to anyone under the age of 30! I have heard millennials say that if they get a phone call, they figure it is some sort of dire emergency on the part of the caller. While Twitter and text messages are fine (probably preferred) for younger people, actually getting an actual e-mail that is not spam is still a treat for me and I fit into the baby boomer demographic.

A few other simple suggestions for serving the newly, or trying to be, retired are as follows:

- Create a Chapter II Advisory Board
- Offer and promote the convenience of e-books
- Consider creating a comfortable, accessible intergenerational space in the children's area, for grandparents and parents to share books with the wee ones
- Offer a special grandparents story hour in the children's department
- Create a mentoring program where experienced older adults can offer their skills and advice to younger people in their areas of expertise
- Set up a volunteer program for the library or keep tabs on other volunteer opportunities in your community through links on the library's website

There are so many small ways in which you can let your devoted older library users know that their patronage over the years is recognized and appreciated and that their experience and knowledge can still be put to good use.

LIBRARY COLLECTIONS AND PROGRAMS

Since you are likely to have a disparate group of older adults using the library, ranging from those desperately hanging on to jobs, some looking for meaningful work to supplement retirement income and others already enjoying or finding ways to enjoy retirement, as with other age groups, it is important to have a mixture of fun programs and collections for the active retiree, as well as being able to incorporate job searching assistance/resume updating types of assistance through programs already in place for those who need it. This younger cohort of still working or newly retired active older adults will be looking for fun and educational programs as they continue to grow at this stage in life.

Catching up on current events or reading for pleasure might be on the recent retiree's list of things that he or she now has time to do. Make sure that you have sufficient copies of current best sellers, both fiction and nonfiction, on hand. Biographies and historical fiction, as well as the more traditional genre fiction, are also popular with older adults, so keep up with the most popular crime/mystery series as well as new Western novels and romances.

When choosing newer titles targeting a particular audience, be sure to display books in areas where they will be noticed and in displays that are appealing and eye-catching. If it is a display on finances in retirement, post a sign that compliments the display and makes it noticeable. I hate general "Staff Picks" displays. How about being a little more specific?

For example, for a display on books about finances in retirement, post a sign with "You've Earned It, Now Enjoy It" along with titles similar to these as follows:

- *Get What's Yours: The Secrets to Maxing Out Your Social Security* by Laurence J. Kotlikoff, Philip Moeller, and Paul Solman
- *Making Social Security Work for You: Advice, Strategies, and Timelines That Can Maximize Your Benefits* by Emily Guy Birken
- *Congratulations on Your Retirement* by Ted Heybridge
- *It's Never Too Late: Getting Older, Wiser, and Worry Free in Our Golden Years* by Scott Page

- *The Retirement Boom: An All Inclusive Guide to Money, Life, and Health in Your Next Chapter* by Catherine Allen and Nancy Bearg
- *Purpose and Power in Retirement* by Harold Koenig
- *70: The New 50* by William Byham

PROGRAMMING FOR LIFELONG LEARNING

In *The Mature Mind: The Positive Power of the Aging Brain*, Dr. Gene Cohen writes about the psychological phases older adults go through.

- Phase I is the midlife reevaluation, which we have already addressed.
- Phase II is the liberation phase, or "If not now, when?" phase.
- Phase III is the summing up phase, where we start to think about our roots, our family history, and recalling life's events, frequently with an entirely new perspective.

With time on their hands, new retirees can once again focus on the things that they would like to do or wish they had done, sometimes delving deeper into family history or taking up writing or some other reflection of the self, such as art, music, or other hobbies. It is probably around retirement age that many people begin to think more about the "summing up" of our lives—our careers, our ancestry—just trying to make sense of it all. Here are some programming ideas for the active older adults age group, continuing their journey of lifelong learning. Always direct participants to areas in the library where they can find information about their particular areas of interest and allow them to "continue the journey" by pointing to community activities, outside websites for exploration, and other groups with similar interests.

Program: Blogging Basics

So many truly wonderful, thoughtful writers have blogs these days. Demonstrate to seniors how to follow a blog and how to set up a blog using websites such as WordPress and Blogger. Encourage them to share their wit and wisdom with the rest of the world.

Suggested readings: *Blogging for Beginners: Learn How to Start and Maintain a Successful Blog the Simple Way* by Terence Lawfield; *WordPress for Dummies* by Lisa Sabin-Wilson; *How to Make Money Blogging: How I Replaced My Day Job with My Blog* by Bob Lotich; and *How to Blog for Profit: Without Selling Your Soul* by Ruth Soukup.

Program: Storytellers

Allow seniors to share personal stories and photos from their own experiences based on various events or times in history within their local community. Locate accompanying materials from the library and find websites, music, and so on to amplify the experience. I have seen this program done in different regions but usually with wonderful results, as each region, each community, and yes, even each person, has a unique story to tell.

Suggested readings: *Ties That Bind: Stories of Love and Gratitude from the First Ten Years of StoryCorps* by Dave Isay; *Mom: A Celebration of Mothers from StoryCorps* by Dave Isay; and *Gather the Fruit One by One: 50 Years of Amazing Peace Corps Stories* by Pat Alter and Bernie Alter.

Art Journaling and Scrapbooking

Art journaling and scrapbooking can be very similar, depending upon a person's artistic ability, or lack thereof. Great artists have made use of art journals for centuries, sketching bits and pieces here and there and jotting down thoughts or feelings or insights into what they are seeing. The great Leonardo da Vinci carried a journal at all times, in which he would record ideas, impressions, and sketches. His journals included invention designs, writings about anatomy, botany, geology, as well as drawings and paintings (http://www.visualjournaling.com/artists.html). For the artistically inclined, a program about art journaling might stir some creative juices and lead to other programs or an exhibit.

For the less artistic, simple scrapbooking is a wonderful and rewarding way of putting together the story of a life, a family's journey, or any number of other ideas. Scrapbooking can be as simple or as complicated as the individual makes it, using personal photos, newspaper or magazine clippings, stickers, and objects. There is an entire industry devoted to scrapbooking. This program could be popular for any age group, but older active adults might really enjoy putting together a family scrapbook or two.

Digital Literacy

Librarians have been bridging the digital divide for seniors for many years now, with wonderful results, but there are still many seniors who continue to need assistance with technology. Having not been "born digital," using technology is something that we (myself included) have had to learn, and libraries can and have assisted many people with technology skills as part of the mission of lifelong learning. According to technology benchmarks established by the Edge Initiative, led by the Urban Libraries Council, at least one of these benchmarks serves to fulfill this purpose, particularly for older adults. The Edge Benchmarks recommend that libraries provide assistance and training to individuals, personalized on-demand technology assistance for 10-minute sessions at all branches, 30-minute sessions by appointment, and one-on-one assistance with personal devices in at least one branch location.

Using these benchmarks as a guideline for serving older adults, as well as immigrant populations, can assist you in determining if your library is meeting the information needs of your local community (http://www .libraryedge.org/benchmarks).

OPPORTUNITIES FOR SERVICE

Since volunteers play such an important role in most libraries and at least some of the newly retired are ripe for the picking, it is in the library's best interest to cultivate a relationship with this demographic.

As I have pointed out in the past, volunteers deserve a planned and organized effort on the part of the library management and staff when they show up to work. Depending upon the person's background and physical capabilities, everyone should have some form of meaningful work to do and policies and procedures in place to ensure that their time in the library goes smoothly. I have had the opportunity to work with wonderful volunteers in more than one position, and from my own experience, volunteers can make a world of difference in any organization. In smaller organizations, volunteers can serve in vital roles, and in larger organizations, the work of volunteers is sometimes just the icing on the cake.

In the interest of finding more quality volunteers, an annual "Tea for the Newly Retired" might be in order. Invite current volunteers to come and mingle and offer up first-hand accounts of what it is like to volunteer at your library. In this instance, especially, be sure that you have treated your volunteers well. In every instance, you should be treating them well. Failing that, a simple listing of "Volunteer Opportunities" on the library web page or posting them on a bulletin board or in a print newsletter is a must. Outreach to local agencies where retirees gather or have some interaction might also be in order. If you are interested in taking the whole volunteer to a new level, VolunteerMatch has formed a partnership with California libraries to support volunteer recruitment efforts in libraries.

Since 2008, VolunteerMatch has partnered with California libraries as part of the Preferred Partnership Program for national nonprofits, where all California library volunteer opportunities are searchable by zip code. The Preferred Partnership Program is available nationwide for a fee. VolunteerMatch staff can use their expertise to conduct symposiums, provide training, provide online webinars and customer support—assist with tracking the number of volunteer referrals, crafting effective post-ings—and provide regular check-ins with volunteer coordinators (http:// blogs.volunteermatch.org/engagingvolunteers/2011/09/13/california-libraries -provide-a-great-example-of-volunteer-engagement/). If you are working with a regional, county, or larger urban library system, it might be worth-while checking in with VolunteerMatch on the possibility of providing a more enhanced volunteer search tool and effective volunteer placement for your library system.

When It Comes to Volunteering, the Size of the Program Does Not Matter

Whether your library has 2 volunteers or 50, there are certain elements, other than getting the volunteers there in the first place, and making sure they feel appreciated while they work, that you should be concerned with. These elements are as follows:

- Volunteer policies
- Volunteer job descriptions and applications
- Background checks
- Volunteer performance evaluations
- Formal appreciation and recognition

While it might be tempting to "take all comers" when it comes to vol-unteer positions, finding the right person for the job can be just as impor-tant, and tricky, as finding the right person for a staff position. Older volunteers with work experience in their background might be easier to place in a volunteer position than younger people on which you might have only personality or affinity for some task with which to make the link to the right job. An application, asking for relevant experience, can help you find the right volunteer for the job. Volunteer applications should follow the same format as a job application, asking for back-ground and experience, information about criminal activity, contact information and previous addresses, and references. Volunteer applica-tions should also state that the applicant understands that they would be working without compensation or benefits as well as the regular certification of honesty in the application. A sample application can be found in Appendix D.

Background Checks

In a recent survey taken by members of the Association for Rural and Small Libraries, my librarian colleagues and I learned that many libraries perform background checks for their volunteers, and probably most libraries perform background checks for certain positions, such as youth and children's services volunteers. Background checks are frequently provided by the parent organization, such as city or county government, including background checks performed by local law enforcement agencies.

CREATING A SPACE FOR SENIORS

About 10 years ago now, my friend and colleague Allan Kleiman, then director of Old Bridge Public Library in Old Bridge, New Jersey, started a new trend, that of "senior spaces" in libraries. Allan figured that since the teens have a space and the children have a dedicated space, why not let the seniors have one? He made his case and received funding to create his own senior space within the Old Bridge library and also made a little library history. Since then, Allan has presented on the topic all across the country and internationally, as well. Allan's interest in and work with seniors long precedes the fame that his senior space brought, but the idea of a senior space is forever associated with Old Bridge Public Library and Allan Kleiman.

While a space completely devoted to seniors might not be in the realm of possibilities for your library, here are a few suggestions for, if not creating a separate senior space, at least approximating one!

1. Choose a quiet corner away from the children and teen areas, and set up a cozy reading space with a couple of chairs, a side table, and a reading lamp. Keep books on subjects of interest to older adults on a shelf nearby. Christen the area with some signage promoting "New Paths from Old" (or any other name) and a location code in the library catalog for the books you keep in the area and voila! You have senior space.

2. Have a special section for the classics in children's literature, books that grandparents would have read as a child and that they might

want to share with the "grands" now. It can be a small shelf in the children's section with a special catalog designation and a rocking chair nearby.

3. Weather permitting, a library should have some sort of outdoor space. It could be a bench near some nice landscaping. It could be an area where gardening takes place. It could be a mentoring opportunity for accomplished older gardeners and kids. If not a library project, local garden clubs would probably love to take on such a project, and having a nice quiet place to take in nature while reading a book could be just what some apartment dwellers are looking for.

MORE DETAILED PROGRAMMING IDEAS

Genealogy for Beginners

It is no wonder that so many older adults become interested in their roots, in learning more about their family history, and the branch that they occupy on the family tree. In *The Mature Mind: The Positive Power of the Aging Brain*, Dr. Gene Cohen suggests that the "summing up phase" in life results from the usage of both sides of the brain, which allows for a deeper understanding of a person's life and that this older, more mature brain, also enjoys reviewing life's events with a deeper understanding. It is a lovely compensation for the things that the body can no longer do, or do as well. Tracing a family's lineage can be a daunting task for the uninitiated, so programs for budding genealogists are always a good bet for older adults.

Learning goals:

- Learn about locating census and death records online.
- Discover web resources where genealogists share family research and information.
- Learn about "destinations" for genealogical research.
- Learn about using local government records like land, marriage, court and even local church records to fill in some blanks.

Steps to take:

- Partner with a local genealogical society to do a short series.
- Locate a presenter or presenters through local history or genealogy society.
- Divide the segments up into shorter one-hour programs.

- Try to offer each segment twice, once during the week and once on the weekend.
- Demonstrate free online websites for genealogy research, such as FamilySearch.org, Cyndi's List, and the USGenWeb Project.
- Be sure to include subscription services like Ancestry.com if the library has a license, or demonstrate the free-trial version.
- Advertise through e-mail lists, the library website, and conventional newsletters and posters on the library bulletin board.
- Have staff take registration for each program and provide a computer lab when needed as much of this information will be found online.

Genealogists are the most sharing people I have ever met. They will share, even when you do not want them to, and many of them are retired and willing to share their knowledge at little or no cost to your library. Enthusiastic about the subject matter, local history buffs and genealogists will help you grow a genealogy program in no time.

Suggested readings:

- *Unofficial Guide to FamilySearch.org: How to Find Your Family History on the Largest Free Genealogy Website* by Dana McCullough
- *How to Do Everything: Genealogy*, Fourth Edition, by George G. Morgan; *Advanced Genealogy Research Techniques* by George G. Morgan and Drew Smith
- *Genealogy Research: How to Organize the Notes, Papers, Documents, Emails, Scans, Computer Files, and Photographs* by D. M. Kalten
- *The Family Tree Problem Solver: Tried-and-True Tactics for Tracing Elusive Ancestors* by Marsha Hoffman Rising and Sharon DeBartolo Carmack

Turn That Passion into $$

Having never been one to say, "I don't know what I would do in retirement," I cannot identify with that mind-set, but I certainly know people who feel that way. Encouraging the newly retired in the community to start afresh with pursuing a lifelong goal would make a great program. Many, many people end up in careers that were not exactly what they were hoping for. With a little retirement income coming in, and time on their hands, making dreams come true during the "golden years" can make them really golden, in more ways than one.

Learning goals:

- Learn from local business people, artists, or craftsmen how to get into the biz.
- Get back in touch with whatever that dream might have been and start exploring it again.
- Learn about advertising and selling through websites like Etsy and Craigslist.

Steps to take:

- Consider offering this program as a short series of three to four presentations.
- Invite local start-up business owners or people who work from home for budding entrepreneurs. Invite crafts people, artists, and musicians for the artistically aspiring individuals.
- Locate people who have made a second career out of consulting in their chosen field.

Suggested readings:

- *The Start of Something BIG: or How to Find an Idea to Make Money* by Maureen Larter and Rachel Mizer
- *The Career Guide for Creative and Unconventional People* by Carol Eikleberry, PhD, and Carrie Pinsky
- *The Savvy Crafters Guide to Success: Turn Your Crafts into a Career* by Sandy McCall and *Turn Your Passion into Profit* by Walt F. J. Goodridge

CONCLUSION

Active seniors can and will continue to use library resources and attend programs, if you can find the right fit to keep their interest, and only you can determine what that might be. If you have the luxury, create a separate senior space for these loyal library supporters. If a full-blown senior space is not in the library's budget or space allocation, carving out a small corner dedicated to the use of older adults is not only a nice gesture but could be a welcome service. Offering a variety of programs, including more in-depth technology classes, will increase your chances of drawing in new users and ultimately offer a better idea of what works or does not work in your community.

CHAPTER 8

Reflecting upon Life's Journey: Age Group 75 and Beyond

Many older adults find in themselves a desire to not only continue to develop around themes and ideas that they have created throughout their lives, as suggested by Dr. Gene Cohen in *The Mature Mind: The Positive Power of the Aging Brain*, but also to spend time in reflection and "summing up" the many facets of their lives. Library programs built around oral histories, journaling, and local history can be of great interest to this demographic. As people live longer, there is ample opportunity for aging adults to take part in library events, and make use of online and books by mail services. As more tech-savvy younger seniors age, more and more of the aging demographic will make use of e-books and online resources, as well. The convenience of checking out a book on the smartphone just holds too much allure, even for die-hard print readers like me. At some point, reading electronic books and magazines on a personal device at home could become a terrific substitute for a trip to the library for some older adults. Making sure that our older adults know how to access online resources is a must for libraries.

According to *65+ in the United States: 2010 Special Studies Current Population Reports* by Loraine A. West, Samantha Cole, Daniel Goodkind, and Wan He, the number of people age 75 and older has increased from 1 percent to 4.2 percent in the last century. The population age 85 and older has grown 9 times in the same time period, and the number of people living beyond 90 years of age is expected to quadruple from 2010 to 2050 (https://www.census.gov/content/dam/Census/library/publications/2014/demo/p23-212.pdf). There is no doubt that people are living longer and consequently can have longer relationships with their local library. Providing useful services and programs for the older population is part of a library's mission to serve an entire community.

LIBRARY SERVICES TO OLDER ADULTS

Because the older population can have particular needs, there are a number of services a library can offer that will have significant impact on their golden years. Some of these suggestions are simple courtesy services and are easy enough to allow current staffing to handle, such as the following:

- Assistance with carrying out books
- Shopping bags or free totes to make carrying books easier
- Referrals to social services
- Assistance with filling out online requests to use community rooms or spaces, if seniors have difficulty
- Reserve aisle seats for program attendees 75+ for convenience and health issues
- Assistance with signing up for programs or allowing "early bird" registration to older adults

Having a "place," whether it is a specific desk, or just the understanding that seniors can go to the circulation or reference desk to ask for concierge or courtesy services, such as assistance with carry-out or advanced registration for a program, is offering a specialized and meaningful service to older adults.

OUTREACH TO INSTITUTIONS AND IN-HOME LIBRARY SERVICES

Providing reading and other materials to people who are unable to come into the library is a service that is most in keeping with one of the primary practices of the profession—to provide services to the entire community, including people unable to visit the library. Many libraries provide outreach services to people in assisted living facilities, nursing homes, adult daycare centers, and even in their homes. Whether this service is accomplished through books by mail to homebound individuals or onsite visits to institutional facilities, it stills falls under the umbrella of outreach services. Outreach to other types of institutions will be discussed in the following chapter.

Traditional In-Home Library Service

In-home library services offer library access to many people who cannot physically get to the library, including those with physical disabilities and the elderly. Many libraries provide delivery and pick-up of library materials to individuals and nursing or assisted living facilities. While offering in-home library service is time, staff, and budget consuming, libraries have an obligation to offer such services to all members of their communities. As stated in the Homebound Program Toolkit, published by the North Texas Library Partners in 2011, there are many compelling reasons to provide this type of service:

- People with disabilities have the same right to access library programs, materials, and services as all other members of a library's community.
- Libraries are grounded in the tradition of providing unfettered access to information and have taken on the challenge of making our buildings, materials, and electronic resources accessible for everyone.
- Providing outreach to homebound individuals takes accessibility a step closer to achieving Universal Access (UA).
- Our population is aging.
- People are living longer and surviving diseases and injuries that previously would have been fatal.
- Extended military conflicts mean that more veterans are returning home with one or more disabilities.
- Most people will experience temporary or permanent disability at some point in their lives.
- Serving this growing demographic is a way for libraries to remain relevant to their communities.
- Those who cannot easily leave their homes are often the people who have the highest need for access to library materials and services.
- Homebound programs often involve partnerships with other organizations, volunteer groups, and service providers, which increases a library's visibility and promotes goodwill between organizations (http://nottypical.org/downloads/FY2011/homebound/HB%20Toolkit%202011.pdf).

Personal Delivery Programs

Personal delivery programs have many advantages for the library user but perhaps more disadvantages to the library itself. The programs are

- much more user friendly for the participants, providing personal contact and an opportunity for interacting with the delivery person,

- a "good will" service in the community,
- based on staff or volunteer interaction with other organizations such as senior centers, assisted living centers, nursing homes, and individuals, and
- a means of increasing library visibility within the community.

All that is being said, this type of personal delivery program involves additional costs, staff time, and liabilities that books by mail programs do not generate. There are liabilities to consider when planning for in-home delivery service such as insurance coverage and background checks for volunteers. It is important to know who you are sending into a person's home. A plan of action for emergency situations in a library patron's home should also be in place.

Library Service by Mail

The Mid-Continent Public Library (MCPL) system, serving three counties in Missouri, offers Library by Mail services, which includes access to not only books but also audiobooks on CD, music on CD, and DVDs delivered to "patrons who cannot get to a library branch because of health, mobility, advanced age, permanent or temporary incapacity." A dedicated reader's advisor will suggest titles based on the readers interest, or users of the service can place orders for specific materials. MCPL allows for application to the program online or by mail, but certification in writing is required from a medical professional for use of the service.

MCPL also lists the following policies regarding the Library by Mail service on the library website:

- Eligibility: Must be a resident of the MCPL district.
- Checkout: Up to 25 items per month. 20 items at one time. 6 week checkout.
- Renewals: Materials can be renewed twice for an additional six weeks per renewal. No notification is needed, renewals are automatically granted for you!
- Overdues: There are no overdue fines! You will be contacted by phone or letter if your materials are seriously overdue.
- Lost and Damaged Materials: Lost and damaged materials are noted in our records and you will be notified by mail. Excessive instances of lost or damaged materials may result in reduction and/or suspension of service.

If a Library by Mail service is beyond the scope of what your library is able to offer, due to staffing or budget constraints, be aware that the National Library Service for the Blind and Physically Handicapped (NLS) offers recorded books and descriptive videos by mail free to persons who qualify for the service. Qualification for NLS services entails notification from a physician that a person is unable to read tradition print materials because of a physical or visual disability. Find out more about the service as well as a list of all of the state and regional libraries of the NLS, which actually provide the service to state and regional library users at http://www.loc.gov/nls.

You can find an example of a public library at home library service application in the Appendix E.

E-Books and E-Readers

E-readers and e-books are a wonderful option for older adults, offering convenience in carrying multiple books at a time and the option to make text larger, brighter, or darker, thereby increasing legibility. As a recent convert to e-books myself, I can attest to the convenience and freedom from strain to shoulders and neck by carrying one small device in my purse instead of two or three books in a bag. Having sworn that I would never give up print and paper, when I moved to a bigger city and started commuting by public transportation, I soon realized that reading an e-book on my smartphone was the ideal solution for me. Older adults, once taught how to use a dedicated e-reader or to download e-books onto a smartphone might greatly appreciate this service. I even recently read all 774 pages of Donna Tartt's *The Goldfinch* on my phone. My vision was blurry for a couple of days, but I was able to snag the book in e-format and gobble it up with my eyes in no time. Put forth an extra effort to make sure your older library users know how to use e-books and e-readers! They can save an aching back or shoulder and a trip to the library when a person just cannot get out of the house.

ASSISTIVE TECHNOLOGY AND COMPUTER ENHANCEMENTS

In *Making Your Web Site Senior Friendly*, the National Institute on Aging provides a list of following suggestions for making the library's website easier to read for people with low vision:

- Use a sans serif typeface, such as Helvetica, that is not condensed. Always avoid the use of serif, novelty, and display typefaces

- Use 12-point or 14-point type size for body text
- Use medium or bold-face type
- Present body text in both uppercase and lowercase letters and reserve underlining for links
- Double-space all body text
- Left-justify blocks of text
- Avoid yellow, blue, and green in close proximity
- Ensure that text and graphics display correctly on a black and white monitor
- Use dark type or graphics against a light background
- Avoid patterned backgrounds
- Write in clear, simple language
- Provide an online glossary of technical terminology
- Break lengthy documents into shorter segments
- Use text-relevant images only
- Provide text alternatives such as open captioning or access to a static version of text for everything animated, video and audio

Other suggestions for layout and design can be found in the same online publication at https://www.nlm.nih.gov/pubs/checklist.pdf.

Readability is a free reading platform that aims to deliver a great reading experience wherever you are and to provide a system to connect readers to the writers they enjoy. Readability can easily be downloaded onto a single computer for seniors to use within the library or at home. It is also available as an app for Android, iPad, iOS, and Mac. When activated, Readability presents a decluttered version of any web page that they are viewing. It removes ads and any confusing Flash, leaving just the text of the web page for clean reading. Web content can be resized for better viewing using the Readability platform.

The American Federation for the Blind offers a number of tips for optimizing visual computer capability with Windows including as follows:

- Windows Ease of Access Center
- Tips for Web Browsing
- Windows Magnifier Screen Magnification Program
- Windows Narrator Screen Reader

Make sure that library staff are aware of these functions and can assist low-vision library users with them, when necessary (http://www.afb.org/info/living-with-vision-loss/using-technology/using-a-computer/part-ii-

for-the-experienced-computer-user-with-a-new-visual-impairment/
windows-accessibility-options/12345).

COLLECTION DEVELOPMENT AND PROGRAMS

A 2005 report *NLS: That All May Read Digital Talking Book Distribution Analysis* by NLS, shows that mysteries are the most popular fiction genre distributed by the NLS, followed by romance, biography, and historical fiction. While there are certainly older adults who will have interest in many other genres, keeping large print and audio versions of these four genres will be appreciated by older library users (http://www .loc.gov/nls/technical/distribution/section-2.html).

A Diversity and Outreach Column posted by ALA's Office of Diversity, Literacy and Outreach Services, reprinted Kansas City Public Library's top authors requested by older library users, broken down by age groups.

Kansas City Public Library (KCPL) readers over the age of 85 most often requested following authors:

1. Maeve Binchy
2. Belva Plain
3. Rosamunde Pilcher
4. LaVyrle Spencer
5. Louis L'Amour
6. Zane Grey
7. Jan Karon
8. Jimmy Carter
9. Margaret Truman
10. Phyllis Whitney

For ages 64–84, the most requested authors were as follows:

1. Barbara Taylor Bradford
2. Tim LaHaye
3. Robert B. Parker
4. Fern Michaels
5. James Patterson
6. Janet Dailey
7. Sandra Brown
8. Patricia Cornwell
9. Catherine Coulter
10. Walter Mosley

This publication also reported that baby boomers reading tastes seemed to reflect a taste for more fast-paced thrillers and accept more sex, violence, and profanity in their reading. The most requested authors for the baby boomers at KCPL at this time were as follows:

1. Stephen King
2. Anne Rice
3. Nora Roberts
4. Dean Koontz
5. Suzanne Brockmann
6. Janet Evanovich
7. Terry McMillan
8. Jonathan Kellerman
9. David Baldacci
10. Richard North Patterson

It is safe to say that many new authors have arrived on the literary scene since the referenced publication, but the preference for genres and tastes in reading probably still hold true (http://olos.ala.org/columns/?p=264).

JOURNALING AND ORAL HISTORY PROJECTS

An old African proverb says that when an elder dies, an entire library is gone. I would have to agree that certainly the most extensive collection of information about an individual's life is gone at that point, and with it, sometimes untold stories. Programs that provide the elderly an opportunity to tell their stories are a wonderful way to engage with both the individual and the community. Putting these stories together in the form of a book or exhibit allows you to share the life's stories of people from your community in a public forum.

Depending upon the size of your community, you could either focus on specific historical events around which people might gather recollections for written or oral history projects, pick local leaders in the community to do a program, or just allow people to focus on their life's stories in their entirety through journaling, oral history or photo exhibits. The size and scope of the project will depend upon your area, your budget, and the people involved.

From my experience with an oral history project for a small historical museum in Western Colorado, I can tell you that such a project can be accomplished on a smaller scale using only volunteers for doing the interviews and transcribing and indexing the recorded sessions. Because of the size of the local population and rich local history to be found on the western slopes of the Colorado Rocky Mountains, the Frontier Historical Society and Museum in Glenwood Springs, Colorado, had an ongoing oral history project when I was director there. The program was implemented with volunteer interviewers and served to record the lives of local artists, political figures, business owners, and other prominent members of the community. The Houston Public Library is a good example of oral history on a grander scale. The Houston Public Library Oral History Project includes the following:

- The Mayor Bill White Collection: Mayor White commissioned 100 initial interviews, directing that it include well-known political, business, and civic leaders, and witnesses to the history of Houston. The interviews are part of the digital archives of the Houston Public Library.
- The Neighborhood Voices tapes: In the summer of 2008, citizens came to Houston Public Library locations throughout the city to record their own brief recollections about life in Houston.
- HMRC Oral Histories: The Houston Metropolitan Research Center of the Houston Public Library recently digitized more than 200 oral histories from the 1970s and 1980s and contains interviews with artists, musicians, civil rights activists, politicians, and civic leaders who helped define the growth and history of the city.
- Building Houston Oral History Project: This collection is the result of a partnership between the William R. Jenkins Architecture and Art Library, a branch of the University of Houston Libraries, and the Houston Chapter of the American Institute of Architects and focuses on the architecture and buildings in the city. To see some of the oral history interviews from Houston Public Library, visit http://www.houstonoralhistory.org/index.html.

Nailing the Oral History Interview

According to the Oral History Association (OHA) at Georgia State University, there are a number of things interviewers can do to make the interview, and resulting collection, more meaningful and useful. In "Best Practices for Oral History," OHA suggests, in a broad sense that "All those who use oral history interviews should strive for intellectual honesty and the best application of the skills of their discipline. They should avoid stereotypes, misrepresentations, and manipulations of the narrator's words. This includes foremost striving to retain the integrity of the narrator's perspective, recognizing the subjectivity of the interview, and interpreting and contextualizing the narrative according to the professional standards of the applicable scholarly disciplines. Finally, if a project deals with community history, the interviewer should be sensitive to the community, taking care not to reinforce thoughtless stereotypes. Interviewers should strive to make the interviews accessible to the community and where appropriate to include representatives of the community in public programs or presentations of the oral history material." More specific suggestions for oral history interviews include these tips:

- Prepare to ask informed questions by conducting background research on the person, topic, and larger context in both primary and secondary sources.
- When ready to contact a possible narrator, send an introductory letter outlining the general focus and purpose of the interview via regular mail or e-mail, and then follow up with either a phone call or a return email, or when other conditions make it appropriate, via face-to-face meetings.
- Schedule a nonrecorded meeting, which will allow an exchange of information between interviewer and narrator on possible questions/topics, reasons for conducting the interview, share information about the process involved, and the need for informed consent and legal release forms.
- Most importantly, "Make sure that the narrator understands oral history's purposes and procedures in general and of the proposed interview's aims and anticipated uses, his or her rights to the interviews including editing, access restrictions, copyrights, prior use, royalties, and the expected disposition and dissemination of all forms of the record, including the potential distribution electronically or on-line, that his or her recording(s) will remain confidential until he or she has given permission via a signed legal release." There are legal issues involved in having access to oral history recordings.
- Use the best digital recording equipment available to reproduce the narrator's voice accurately and, if appropriate, other sounds and visual images, if video equipment is available. Before the interview, interviewers should become familiar with the equipment and be knowledgeable about its function.
- Always prepare an outline of interview topics and questions to use as a guide to the recorded dialogue.

- Obviously, the interview should be conducted in a quiet room with little or no background noises and possible distractions.
- Recording a "lead" at the beginning of each session to help focus the narrator's thoughts to each session's goals, consisting of, at least, the names of narrator and interviewer, day and year of session, interview's location, and proposed subject of the recording.
- Both parties should agree to the approximate length of the interview in advance, but, in particular, in the case of elderly narrators, the interviewer is responsible for assessing whether the narrator is becoming tired and offers a stopping point or rest period. Although most interviews last about two hours, if the narrator wishes to continue those wishes should be honored, if possible.
- Along with asking creative and probing questions and listening to the answers to ask better follow-up questions, the interviewer should conduct the interview in accordance with any prior agreements made with narrator, which should be documented for the record.
- Interviewers should work to achieve a balance between the objectives of the project and the perspectives of the interviewees and fully explore all appropriate areas of inquiry with interviewees. Superficial responses do not make a good oral history. At the same time, encourage narrators to respond to questions in their own style and language and to address issues that reflect their concerns.
- Interviewers must respect the rights of interviewees to refuse to discuss certain subjects, to restrict public access to the interview, or even to choose anonymity. Interviewers should clearly explain these options to all interviewees.
- Strive to record candid information of lasting value.
- Always secure a release form, by which the narrator transfers his or her rights to the interview to the repository or designated body, signed after each recording session or at the end of the last interview with the narrator.

For more information about oral history projects and pre- and post interview tips, visit http://www.oralhistory.org/about/principles-and-practices.

Journaling Programs

Harris County Library in Texas, with branches in the Houston area, has a program called "Journaling in the Library" (http://www.hcpl.net/content/journaling-library-2). This ongoing program relies on writing prompts to inspire would be autobiographers to get busy! If there are reluctant writers among your seniors who have stories that should be told, maybe journaling would provide the impetus to get those pens moving.

Journaling can be both therapeutic and assist with recall. Seniors who journal may wish to keep their thoughts private or pass them down as a legacy to other family members. Writing can be a way to work through feelings and memories of the past or deal with present-day stress, fears, hopes, or even dreams of the future. They can be a way to track goals and develop strategies for achieving progress on their personal bucket lists.

Journals can be handwritten, be typed, or use other technological aids, such as tape recorders, video equipment on phones, and other devices, for those who have difficulty writing or seeing. Monthly journaling groups can keep writers motivated and allow them to share ideas and content. Books, guest lectures, visual aids, and examples of other journals can help get your group started, jump start ideas, or allow them to progress beyond a writer's block.

For those who prefer handwritten journals, allow writers to unlock their creativity with things like colored pencils, stickers, markers and other expressive writing tools to make their journals more beautiful and expressive. Some seniors may prefer to journal exclusively through artistic rendering. Allowing them access to art supplies in house or to borrow supplies to take home can help facilitate their creative journeys.

LOCAL HISTORY DISPLAYS AND PROGRAMMING

Journaling and oral history projects can lead to some creative display opportunities and programming options in the library, focusing on local history, if participants are willing to share their stories.

One of the best attended programs we hosted at the Frontier Historical Society, in conjunction with the local public library in Glenwood Springs, Colorado, was with a group of older gentlemen who referred to themselves as "The Romeos," or "Retired Old Men Eating Out." This group of four to five retired men would get together once a month and tell stories of this area, which was on the western slopes of the Rocky Mountains, near Aspen. The area, originally settled by the Ute people, had been host to outlaws and politicians, dignitaries and diplomats, was a late nineteenth-century spa, known for its hot springs pool, and a ski area. There were many stories to tell, and the local community loved to share them. Putting together a panel discussion of some historical event or period in a community's history is usually a winning program.

Almost everyone has old photos that they love to share. Frequently, people have artifacts that they would like to exhibit. While collecting artifacts is out of most libraries' scope, some libraries do indeed have artifact collections, and many have photo collections. If planning a photo or archive exhibit is in your future plans and your experience with historical collections are limited, listed further are a few things to consider in preparation for the exhibit.

Security

If planning for a short-term exhibit, three to four weeks, of photographs or artifacts related to local history, security is most likely going to be an area of concern. While exhibiting items or photos for an extended period of time requires some attention to preserving and protecting the items from damaging light or other environmental factors, hosting a short-term exhibit should not create great cause for concern. Having a secure case for the exhibit and permission to publicly display the items will be the main concern, particularly if the items have any monetary value. Prior to having a security system, Native American artifacts were stolen from the previously mentioned local history museum in Colorado. The handmade cases were covered in Plexiglas and held in place by screws. Some enterprising thieves were able to unscrew the screws and take the artifacts while unsuspecting volunteers sat at the information desk on another floor. When planning an exhibit, make sure that your library has sufficient security measures in place to protect artifacts and documents, or use reproductions only. No one wants to loan the library their ancestor's Civil War sword for an exhibit, only to have it come up missing.

Display Housing

If using built-in display cabinets, make sure that they are equipped with locks, and house the keys away from the display cases. Check the security of the cases even while locked. I recently had a patron demonstrate for me how he could open a locked display case, just by lifting up on the doors of the case. He was quite proud of himself, too. If doors are loose or locks broken, have the repair work done before the exhibit opens.

If borrowing or using any type of portable display case, similar to display cases with sliding back doors found in department stores, ensure that the cases have a locking mechanism or get permission to have some type of lock installed, even if it is only a padlock on the sliding doors. Check that all of the glass panels are sealed or attached to the cabinet itself, not just sitting on top of the cabinet, where it can be lifted off without any trouble. Providing a sense of security for anyone loaning items for display or for your own collections is mandatory.

Borrowers and Lenders

When borrowing items, something of equal importance to providing real security for the items is having some form of agreement in place. Depending upon the value of the item, insurance might be necessary or even required by local governing agencies. A simple photo exhibit would not require the kind of security or insurance as that Civil War sword, but loan agreements are recommended for any original items, including documents or photos, and, of course, good copies can be made for exhibit purposes.

A borrower's agreement can be a simple one page document between the lender, which could be an individual or another institution, and the library, or borrower. The agreement should specify an amount of time in which the item will be on loan, either in weeks or in terms of from one specific date to another. The agreement should also state that the borrower is responsible for the care and preservation of the item while it is in the borrower's care, at a minimum. By the same token, if lending items for display from your library's collection, be sure to have a lending agreement in place with the borrowing institution.

Other Notes on Local Displays

As I have noted in the past, libraries can often become unwitting collectors of a community's *stuff*. When people showed up at the local historical society with items that did not fall under the scope of our collection, I would often direct them to the local public library. At one library where I worked, we had a lovely display case, donated by a library patron, but specifically given to us to display the numerous items that he and his wife collected during their travels, such as clay donkeys, hula girls, and Russian nesting dolls. Do not fall into such a trap! A Deed of Gift spelling out the library's rights to use any gift, without restriction, and to dispose of gifts when necessary, is a must. It is too easy to just accept someone's generosity *with strings attached*, especially in smaller communities where feelings might be hurt or toes stepped on.

MORE DETAILED PROGRAMMING IDEAS

Focus on Wellness

While health and well-being is important at any age, paying extra attention to our bodies and understanding what is going on with them becomes crucial to the elderly. Libraries can play a critical role in the health literacy of older populations of people. Perhaps not being as aware of the number of reliable health resources available to them online, older adults can use a little instruction and guidance for finding good health and wellness resources online and in the library. Since overall wellness embraces a wide range of subjects, "Focus on Wellness" could make up a year-long series for older adults.

Learning goals:

- Become an informed patient
- Become an advocate for your own health
- Learn to find online resources
- Learn to talk to your doctor about concerns and issues
- Learn about alternative medicine
- Learn new "easier on the joints" exercise techniques

Steps to take:

- Locate speakers through local county extension services, colleges, and providers of health services
- Seek out state or regional coordinators of the National Network of Libraries of Medicine (NNLM) for presentations related to NNLM's online resources like MedLine, MedLine Plus, and Center for Disease Control (CDC) online tools
- Review online resources from the NNLM and CDC, and do your own presentation
- Have computer terminals or laptops available for hands-on experience when demonstrating online resources
- Have relevant library materials ready for display and point to online library resources for further information
- Have listings of local health and fitness agencies readily available

Suggested readings/topics:

- *What Patients Say, What Doctors Hear* by Danielle Ofri
- *The Patient's Playbook: Find the "No-Mistake Zone"* by Leslie D. Michelson
- *Your Health, Your Decisions: How to Work with Your Doctor to Become a Knowledge-Powered Patient* by Robert Alan McNutt
- *End Everyday Pain for 50+: A 10-Minute-a-Day Program of Stretching, Strengthening and Movement to Break the Grip of Pain* by Dr. Joseph Tieri

- *The Posture Pain Fix: How to Fix Your Back, Neck and Other Postural Problems That Cause Pain in Your Body* by Rosalind Ferry
- *Medical Terminology: Medical Terminology Made Easy: Breakdown the Language of Medicine and Quickly Build Your Medical Vocabulary* by Eva Regan
- *The Herbal Apothecary: 100 Medicinal Herbs and How to Use Them* by J. J. Pursell
- *Healing Superfoods for Anti-Aging: Stay Younger, Live Longer* by Karen Ansel

Offering up informative programming on health and well-being for seniors creates an opportunity for multiple programs and discussions. Be sure to include as much material and information as you can online, to benefit those who might not be able to attend in-house programs.

Exclusive Preview

Many older adults may not be able to get out to the symphony, opera, or local theater to catch an evening concert or performance. What if you could offer an "Exclusive Preview" for your seniors during the afternoon for upcoming events in the community? It might take some persuading, but providing that you have the space, every performer needs to practice. Invite musicians, artists, and other performers to practice on your seniors, allowing them to talk about the music or play, or even explain a little about the learning process or what goes on behind the scenes. If there is an art exhibit coming up, maybe an artist wants to show off a work of art and talk about the artistic process.

Learning goals:

- Learn about new musical, artistic, or theatrical works
- Learn about artistic processes
- Observe practice habits of musicians and performers
- Learn about library resources on art, music, and theater

Steps to take:

- Offer an honorarium to individual artists or a donation to ensembles
- Frame it as an opportunity to practice before a live audience
- Reach out to local university and college music departments for music students who need performance outlets

- Work with local arts agencies to find artists who would like to share their work
- Keep an eye on the theater scene and try to snag some performers to give a taste of an upcoming production
- Market the "Exclusive Preview" via standard library outlets, and be sure to market the upcoming full productions and concerts, as a courtesy
- Be sure to provide library materials to compliment the performance and continue the learning journey

Suggested reading/topics:

- Biographies of well-known performing and visual artists
- Local histories about local artists and performers, if they exist
- Instructional books on art and music
- Actual music scores or play scripts for more in-depth learning

While not every musician, performer, or artist will have the time to give, be persistent in seeking out these kinds of opportunities for both performer and audience.

CONCLUSION

While older library users do have different needs and interests, much like any other age group, other programming ideas and services suggested in earlier chapters can be tailored to meet the older adults' needs. Making sure that older patrons are aware of the convenience that new technologies can provide, such as recorded or e-books online, and insuring that they can use these technologies is a wonderful service that almost all libraries can offer. In this chapter, I offered some specific suggestions for programming, such as oral and local history projects and journaling activities, as well as reading materials for this age group, allowing them to continue on their journey of lifelong learning and sharing. As always, you and your staff are the ones to determine what works best in your community, for your older library users. By doing a little reflection of your own, you can come up with successful services and meaningful programs for this sometimes underserved age group.

CHAPTER 9

Library Service to All

When a library has the mission to serve an entire community, it means just that—the entire community, regardless of race, color, creed, sexual preference, gender preference, or lifestyle. It is not our job to judge or pry into the private lives of those we serve but to provide them with the information that they are seeking, without censure or even overt interest. We provide everyone in our local communities with useful services, no questions asked.

SERVICE TO IMMIGRANT POPULATIONS

According to data from the Pew Research Center, there are 97 counties in the United States in which the former white majority has become the minority, due to lower birth rates among younger Caucasians, aging of the generation of the "big family," and the influx of immigrants to the "Sunbelt" states. While Caucasians still remain the largest single racial group in all but four of these counties, the combination of immigrant and African American populations makes up the majority (http://www.pewresearch.org/fact-tank/2015/04/08/reflecting-a-racial-shift-78-counties-turned-majority-minority-since-2000). Now more than ever, immigrant populations need the services libraries have to offer in the form of English as a Second Language (ESL) assistance, obtaining government information and being on the path to citizenship.

"So what does this mean for my library?" you might be asking yourself.

It means that you have a golden opportunity to reach out to new users who will someday become a big part of the foundation of your library support. It also means that if we ignore these statistics and fail to reach out to immigrant populations, we will *lose* a big part of the foundation of our library support. Every major business concern in the United States has its automated voice system option in Spanish, which says something about how businesses understand and market to this growing demographic. Libraries should be doing the same thing, too.

Different Cultures, Different Perceptions

The Spanish Language Outreach (SLO) program, funded by the Gates Foundation through WebJunction, explored misconceptions about public libraries on the part of Spanish-speaking immigrants, demonstrating that there are frequently "Varying experiences with public libraries in country of origin." Some common misconceptions about public libraries in America, stemming from practices in the immigrant's country of origin, are as follows:

- Public libraries are only for students or people with considerable education.
- Library materials are offered for sale and not loan.
- The word "libreria" in Spanish means "bookstore," and sounds more than a bit like "library," which could account for confusion.
- Access to the library and materials are fee based.
- Libraries might divulge the personal information government agencies, as this could very easily happen in some countries.
- Libraries in America only have English language materials (http://www.webjunction.org/materials/webjunction/Spanish_Language_Outreach_Program_Workshop_Curriculum.html).

These types of misconceptions often discourage new immigrants from coming into the library in the first place, which is a good reason to do outreach to immigrant populations in your community, creating a visible presence for the library where immigrant populations gather, such as churches, local groceries, and social services agencies. Understanding that all immigrants are not familiar with the concept of "free public libraries" gives you impetus to get out of the library and find the people where they are.

Outreach to Spanish Speakers

Spanish is the second most often spoken language in the United States, and Spanish-speaking populations can be found all over the United

States, in both urban and rural areas. As statewide coordinator of the Gates Foundation SLO program for the state of Missouri in 2007–2008, I was privileged to attend training in outreach to Spanish speakers, as well as plan and implement trainings and grant opportunities for Missouri libraries in library services to this ever-growing portion of our population. The SLO program trained over 6,000 library staff via 440 workshops presented in 40 states across the country. The training materials for the SLO program can still be found on WebJunction at http://www .webjunction.org/explore-topics/slo.html, in addition to other resources on outreach to immigrants.

The SLO program stressed the importance of locating and networking with community leaders within the Spanish-speaking community. Each local workshop that we presented in libraries in the state of Missouri required the invitation of local community leaders from the Spanish-speaking community, ideally, such as ministers and business owners, or the presence of individuals who worked with the community, such as social workers, ESL teachers, and other professionals from the community. In these workshops, we learned that working to ensure the trust and friendship of local leaders in the Spanish-speaking community is key to earning the trust of the general population. This simple practice is one that could be applied to any immigrant community. Identifying and reaching out to community leaders is key to building a relationship with immigrants. Start by doing the following:

- Invite community leaders to be part of an outreach to immigrant populations committee at the library. Community leaders in the Spanish-speaking population are considered to be the "gate keepers" and can be the conduit to your success in introducing library services to this demographic.
- Go where the people are with information about the library and its services. This could include the local laundromat, schools, churches, social services offices, immigrations centers, and even restaurants. Ask to post flyers or drop-off pamphlets about what the library has to offer.
- Ask to do presentations at churches, in schools, social clubs, or ESL classes. Teaching new immigrants about library resources is a way to ensure that they become library users and supporters on their way to citizenship.
- Post signage or have library information in as many languages used in your community as your available resources will allow.

The Library 101

Immigrant populations often need an introduction to the free libraries of America. In some countries, a free library simply does not exist. By creating and offering a Library 101 course, you can provide a brief, but thorough, introduction to the library and its resources. Making this a "traveling show" is a must. Take your Library 101 introductory course out to churches, community centers, assistance centers, anywhere that immigrants might congregate and need to know about the library's offerings. Have a volunteer translator on hand to overcome the language barriers. New immigrants to the United States will most likely be open and receptive to your message, once they understand that there are "no strings attached," and new immigrant populations=new library users.

Once you have made contact with and gained the trust of immigrant communities, it is important to have a welcoming and easy to understand system in place to assist people who may or may not speak English, even as a second language. Signage, forms, and instructions printed in the dominant languages of bigger immigrant communities can make for easier communication, once they have found their way into the library.

U.S. Citizenship and Immigration Services

The Department of U.S. Citizenship and Immigration Services (USCIS) offers a wealth of information on the steps to becoming a U.S. citizen as well as a free downloadable booklet for starting a citizenship program in your local community. USCIS recognizes the important role that libraries currently play and have historically played in the assimilation of new immigrants into our culture and assistance on the path to citizenship. As recognized in Library Services for Immigrants: A Report on Current Practices, a 2009 report published by USCIS with funding from the Institute of Museum and Library Services, "Public libraries in the United States have a long history of providing resources and education to immigrants. This tradition may be traced to Andrew Carnegie's support for public libraries as a place for immigrant self-education, enlightenment, and the study of democracy and English." Keeping with this tradition is even more critical in 2016, in light of the current attitudes toward immigrants being expressed by some in the United States.

At USA.gov, recognizing that "Libraries are important community institutions. In the United States, people turn to public libraries as vital sources of information and service referrals. Immigrants often come to libraries for those reasons and to learn about the resources available to help them," links are provided that will help librarians identify resources to assist newcomers on the following:

- Citizenship Resources for Learners, Adult Educators, and Organizations: The Citizenship Resource Center from USCIS provides a one-stop resource for locating information about becoming a U.S. citizen, lesson plans for citizenship classes, and resources for immigrant-serving organizations.
- Free Educational Materials for Immigrant-Serving Organizations: USCIS offers a free Civics and Citizenship Toolkit to immigrant-serving organizations, including public libraries that help prepare immigrants for citizenship. The Toolkit contains educational materials that focus on both naturalization preparation and civic learning.
- Free Materials to Promote Citizenship Education and Awareness: Learn about USCIS' initiative to raise awareness of the rights, responsibilities, and importance of U.S. citizenship. Find posters, radio and video messages, and information on how community organizations, including libraries, can support this effort.
- Find an ESL or Citizenship Class: America's Literacy Directory allows immigrants to search for an English and citizenship class in their local area. If your library offers classes or programs, we encourage you to add them to the directory.
- Examples of Citizenship Education Initiatives in Public Libraries: The Los Angeles Public Library established "citizenship corners" in each of their branches containing essential information for those looking to apply for citizenship or learn more about the benefits and responsibilities of being a U.S. citizen.
- The Queens Library includes a "Citizenship and Immigration" section on its website, which provides a list of community resources available to immigrants. The library also has a New Americans Program highlighting services, programs, and resources the library provides to immigrants.
  The Hartford Public Library's website includes an "Immigration and Citizenship" section with information on the services it provides to immigrants.
- E-mail Alerts on Citizenship and Citizenship Education: Sign up to receive free email alerts from USCIS with important news and information on a variety of topics.

Citizenship Corners in Libraries

The USCIS encourages libraries, as integral parts of their local communities, to establish a digital and physical "Citizenship Corner" in the library. These Citizenship Corners provide a dedicated space in your library where immigrants can find information about becoming a U.S. citizen. USCIS has developed educational materials to help prepare individuals for naturalization. Here immigrants can find the information and resources they need to start the path toward becoming a U.S. citizen.

A typical Citizenship Corner includes citizenship test preparation materials along with information about the naturalization process. Libraries can also add information about community resources, English teaching materials, and other relevant books and videos from their collections. While there are a number of immigration topics that may be of interest to libraries and their customers, USCIS recommends displaying only citizenship and naturalization-related resources in the Citizenship Corner. The USCIS offers the following helpful suggestions for establishing a Citizenship Corner in your library:

- Order one free copy of the USCIS Civics and Citizenship Toolkit. The Toolkit contains immigration and civics publications, handbooks, and multimedia tools, such as the USCIS Naturalization Interview and Test video, Quick Civics Lessons for the Naturalization Test, Vocabulary Flash Cards for the Naturalization Test, Civics Flash Cards for the Naturalization Test (English and Spanish), and Civics and Citizenship Multimedia Presentation.
- Download Form N-400, Application for Naturalization and provide copies in the Citizenship Corner. (Remind your customers that all USCIS forms are free.)
- Display and distribute free USCIS informational resources.
- Print 11" × 17" citizenship awareness posters in English, Chinese, Spanish, and Vietnamese. Display these posters in the Citizenship Corner, classrooms, and other visible areas.
- Print 6" × 9" informational flyers in English, Chinese, Spanish, and Vietnamese. These flyers highlight naturalization eligibility requirements and resources available on the USCIS Citizenship Resource Center.
- Download and distribute the brochure of 10 Steps to Naturalization: Understanding the Process of Becoming a U.S. Citizen.

- Download and display the Pathway to U.S. Citizenship poster.
- Enhance your Citizenship Corner with other citizenship-related and ESL resources from your library's collection.
- Locate the Citizenship Corner near ESL textbooks and resources or post signs directing customers.
- Feature books and magazines that address the content of the 100 civics questions on the naturalization test such as famous Americans, historical events, and important founding documents.
- Arrange your Citizenship Corner to be welcoming and helpful. Here are some additional suggestions:
- Decorate the Citizenship Corner in a patriotic theme.
- Distribute promotional flyers for citizenship or ESL classes offered at your library.
- Distribute flyers from local Board of Immigrant Appeals (BIA) recognized organizations that may be able to help immigrant customers with USCIS forms. Visit uscis.gov for more information on finding legal services and BIA recognized organizations.
- Create and distribute a referral list of local community organizations that provide citizenship services and ESL classes in your community.
- Add computers to the Citizenship Corner and set the Internet browser home page to www.uscis.gov/citizenship, a one-stop USCIS resource for locating citizenship preparation materials and activities.
- Set up a video monitor at the Citizenship Corner and play the USCIS Naturalization Interview and Test video on a continuous loop.
- Set up a computer workstation that displays Preparing for the Oath: U.S. History and Civics for Citizenship at http://americanhistory.si .edu/citizenship. This interactive website highlights museum objects from the Smithsonian Institution to help people prepare for the civics portion of the naturalization test.
- USCIS often hosts naturalization information sessions and administrative naturalization ceremonies in libraries. View the list of upcoming naturalization information sessions at libraries nationwide at https://www.uscis.gov/citizenship/learners/free -information-sessions. Contact your local USCIS community relations officer if you are interested in USCIS hosting a similar session at your library.
- Create a virtual Citizenship Corner on your library website by adding free web resources from https://www.uscis.gov/citizenship/ learners. You may want to add a link on your website.

- Link to USCIS resources by adding a widget to your website. The widgets are small online applications in English and Spanish that can be embedded on social media sites, blogs, or other web pages. Find widgets here: https://www.uscis.gov/citizenship/see-all-section -items-title/Widgets/55247?destination=node/41137
- Get your immigrant library users on the road to citizenship by linking to the "Find Help in Your Community" page on the USCIS Citizenship Resource Center. Another resource for finding community organizations that offer ESL, civics, and citizenship education classes is America's Literacy Directory. Search for programs by zip code.
- To finish off your virtual Citizenship Corner, be sure to include information about immigration and citizenship resources available at your library.

Assisting new immigrants on their path to citizenship is in keeping with the library's mission of serving the entire community and creates an opportunity for the library to provide a service that will have long lasting impact on individual lives, the local community, and the nation.

Technology Assistance to Immigrant Populations

According to a *Library Journal* article titled Many Low-Income Families "Under-Connected" to Internet, Survey Finds, two-fifths have mobile-only Internet access by Linda Jacobson, while many lower-income families have Internet access, a large number of them rely solely on mobile devices for Internet access. Often those with computer access at home are living with slow access, and, in particular, families headed by Hispanic immigrants are the least likely to have online access. (Library Journal. 141.4 (Mar. 1, 2016): p29). With students increasingly relying on Internet access to do research and homework assignments, and with employers only offering online application for jobs, having access to computers and reliable Internet service is a necessity. In this respect, libraries are still bridging the digital divide since the term was first tossed around in the mid-1990s and there continues to be a demand for computers in libraries.

The Edge Benchmarks for technology, referenced in previous chapters, suggest that libraries offer technology assistance in other languages in at least one branch. While this may seem like a tall order for some libraries to fill, particularly the language benchmarks, make an effort to find a native speaker of the most predominant foreign language in your community to assist with translating written instructions into another language, at least in urban areas. Short of hiring multilingual staff, it makes sense that if you have a population speaking another language in your area, you should be able to find a volunteer or contract with someone to assist with the translation issues, if only to create simple instructions and signage for computer terminals.

While learning library terminology of any kind in every language is not feasible, it would be helpful to new immigrants to know a least a few simple library terms in languages that predominate in your area.

E-Government Resources

Edge Benchmarks also lists links to e-government resources as critical in library service, and especially to immigrant populations. Links to local, state, and federal online government services should be part of the library's web presence. Consider providing links to health and social services, housing authority, consumer protection information, state and federal job services, tax forms, and disaster and emergency services, broken out by category of service. At a minimum, provide links to the entry portals for local, state, and federal government pages, which will, in turn, offer more links to the specific on e-government resources online. USA.gov is the official web portal of the federal government and has links to federal government web pages, services, forms, and so on. USA.gov also provides a tool for searching for state government portals at https://www.usa.gov/states-and-territories.

PROGRAMMING FOR IMMIGRANT POPULATIONS

Since there is so much to try to understand when moving to a new country, practical programming highlighting community services, life skills, job searching, and resume writing are essential for many new immigrants.

- A simple program on banking services could be useful, as sometimes immigrants fall prey to check cashing services that charge higher fees, or paycheck loan services that charge exorbitant interest rates.
- Do a simple program highlighting various community services, such as health services, after school programs, and services for families in crisis.

- Find volunteers from within the different immigrant communities to assist with technology classes, resume and job search assistance, and have set conversational English classes weekly. Denver Public Library has an excellent volunteer assisted program with its Plaza services (https://www.denverlibrary.org/services-immigrants).
- "Months" dedicated to programming for specific populations, such as Asian-Pacific heritage month and Hispanic-Latino heritage month. Highlight cuisine, music, art, or other cultural traditions. Involve the local community when planning these types of programs and better your chances of drawing people in.
- Kentucky's Louisville Free Public Library (LFPL) holds monthly Cultural Showcases of presentations, food, live music, dance, games, and elaborate decorations.
- LFPL also provides a venue for immigrant professionals and artists to share their talents with their new community. Facilitated by librarians and patrons, the programs consist of lectures and discussions on literature, film, psychology, philosophy, and sociology, presented to populations that speak the same language from different countries

As new immigrants feel more "at home" in the library, they will soon learn to make use of the library's services and find other programs that would be of interest and beneficial. Programs directly targeted to immigrant populations serve both as a "taste" of what the library has to offer and to assist them in learning more about the community to which they have moved.

Links to Library Resources for Spanish Speakers

The Beaufort County Library put together a *Communication First Aid Kit Bienvenidos a la Biblioteca*, back in 2008, which is still relevant and useful. The entire guide can be found at http://www.webjunction.org/content/dam/WebJunction/Documents/webJunction/Bienvenidos-a-la-Biblioteca!-A-Spanish-Pointing-Guide. The first aid kit includes sample "pointing guides" with side-by-side English and Spanish library terminology, which can be used by anyone, regardless of their understanding of the language. Spanish-speaking information seekers can point to what they are looking for and English-speaking staff will understand. The 61-page guide also offers pronunciation tips, conversational and informational phrases in Spanish and English, Dewey classification in both languages, and sample library location and hour signage as well as sample library forms in Spanish. It is a fairly comprehensive resource for library terminology in Spanish/English and I hope WebJunction will leave it online forever!

For more in depth study of library terminology in Spanish, The Learning Light, LLC, offers an eight-week course in library terminology called "Spanish That Works!". The Missouri State Library purchased multiple licenses for "Spanish That Works!" and offered grants to hire Spanish-speaking trainers to present the course materials at several locations around the state. Large urban libraries made good use of the program and trained a number of staff in library terminology in Spanish. You can find out more about "Spanish That Works!" at http://www.spanishthatworks.org/spanish-for-library-staff, if more than a few words in Spanish is needed at your library or branch.

Providing outreach and services to new immigrant populations ensures that your library would not be missing out on an opportunity for growth.

LIBRARY SERVICES TO THE INCARCERATED

In Prisons & Publics, "Public libraries are providing service to the incarcerated and their families in an effort to ease reentry" (*Library Journal*, February 2017), April Witteveen highlights library outreach programs to the incarcerated in Minnesota, Oregon, Pennsylvania, Utah, New York, and Maryland. While one of the goals of these programs is to assist inmates in reentry into greater society, fostering family literacy is also an important focal point of these public library/prison initiatives.

The Hennepin County Library system in Hennepin County, Minnesota, has had a program called "Read to Me" since 1997. The program allows inmates of the local county jail to record themselves reading a story and then share the recording and the book with the inmates' children. Inmates are also encouraged and taught to continue reading with their children upon release from incarceration. Early in the history of the program, a newsletter and marketing campaign within the jail promoted library services to inmates. Programming within the jail includes writing-based activities such as books reports and emphasis on philosophy and journal reading.

The Free Library of Philadelphia offers Stories Alive, a program providing picture books for inmates to read to their children during family visitation, including participation through Skype. The aim of the program, to promote family literacy and connections between family members, once funded by grants, is part of the library's regular operating budget. The program also includes the circulation of popular and genre fiction and dictionaries, important to the continued growth and development of the inmates themselves.

Salt Lake County Library Services has libraries within the Metro and Oxbow county jails, with a collection of up to 30,000 titles. Books are delivered directly to inmates, and about two-thirds of the collection is in circulation all the time. Library staff there facilitate life-skills classes highlighting library and community resources for inmates prior to their release, including resume and job resources, testing sites, and continuing education resources.

New York Public Library recently opened a 1,200 volume library in the women's facility of the Rikers Island prison complex. The previous method of delivery to inmates was book carts traveling through the prison units, and did not allow for enough access for those seeking access to library resources. Opening an actual facility quadrupled the library's prison patron base as well as allows for literacy-based programming with in the library. One of the more interesting programs offered here is the "Call Me Ishmael" program, which allows readers to leave a voicemail describing a book that made a difference in their lives, which is then transcribed into typewritten animation, as a means of allowing prisoners to share favorite titles.

Library services to the incarcerated are an important step in getting people who have made mistakes in their lives back to their families, back into society, and into the workplace. If starting a prison/library partnership is something of interest in your area, learning more from these great examples would be beneficial.

LIBRARY SERVICES TO PEOPLE WITH DISABILITIES

The term "disability" is applied to any number of conditions affecting human beings. Many people identified as having disabilities prefer not to think of themselves as disabled, at all; perhaps just different in some way, much like all of us are different in many ways. Having been the Adult Services Consultant for the Missouri State Library, I worked with various agencies to provide training in the area of library services to people with disabilities, in addition to outreach to Spanish speakers, and it was through this work that I learned of the "People First" movement. Too often we find ourselves thinking and speaking of the perceived disability first, and the person second, using phrases like, "handicapped people" or "disabled people." But we should always remember that people with disabilities are people, first and foremost, and they like to be identified as such. Consequently, there is a movement dedicated to recognizing people with disabilities as people first and some helpful language that goes along with the movement. Here are some examples of "people first" language:

Say	Instead of
person with a disability	handicapped, disabled
person with a congenital disability	person with a birth defect
person who has been diagnosed with …	person afflicted with or suffers from
person who has Down syndrome	Downs person, mongoloid, mongol
person who has been diagnosed with autism	the autistic
person with quadriplegia	quadriplegic
person with a physical disability	a cripple
people who are blind, person who is visually impaired	the blind
person with a learning disability	learning disabled
person diagnosed with a mental health condition	crazy, insane, and mentally ill

Always identify the person first and the particular condition second, if at all, much the same way that we use other characteristics, like brown eyes, or height, or hair color to identify each other. The People First movement is an international organization that promotes self-advocacy for people with disabilities. For more information about People First, visit http://www.peoplefirst.org.

Another wonderful website for advocacy for people with disabilities is https://www.disabilityisnatural.com, hosted by mother, advocate, and motivational speaker Kathie Snow. Part of Kathie's message is clear from the name of her newsletter and web page, "Disability is Natural." Realizing that physical and mental differences exist in all of us, and makes each of us unique, Snow champions the idea that people with disabilities are just unique individuals, an inspiring message to champion. In an effort to serve the entire community, libraries should put forth a real effort to ensure that people with disabilities can use the library's resources, just like everyone else.

Visual Accessibility

Many older, as well as younger, adults are visually impaired and find computer use difficult. While following these guidelines set out by the National Institute of Health on making your website senior friendly may not be as exciting as you would like, making the information found on your website accessible to everyone is important. In "Making Your Web Site Senior Friendly," the National Institute on Aging and the National Library of Medicine make the following suggestions for making your website easier to read and understand for everyone:

- Use a sans serif typeface, such as Helvetica, that is not condensed. Avoid the use of serif, novelty, and display typefaces.
- Use 12-point or 14-point type size for body text.
- Use medium or bold-face type.
- Present body text in uppercase and lowercase letters. Use all capital letters and italics in headlines only. Reserve underlining for links.
- Double space all body text.
- Left justified text is optimal for older adults.
- Avoid yellow, blue, and green in close proximity. These colors and juxtapositions are difficult for some older adults to discriminate. Ensure that text and graphics are understandable when viewed on a black and white monitor.
- Use dark type or graphics against a light background, or white lettering on a black or dark-colored background. Avoid patterned backgrounds.
- Present information in a clear and familiar way to reduce the number of inferences that must be made. Use positive statements.
- Use the active voice.
- Write the text in simple language.
- Provide an online glossary of technical terms.
- Organize the content in a standard format.
- Break lengthy documents into short sections.
- Use text-relevant images only.
- Use short segments to reduce download time on older computers.
- Provide text alternatives such as open-captioning or access to a static version of the text for all animation, video, and audio.
- Carefully label links.
- Use explicit step-by-step navigation procedures whenever possible to ensure that people understand what follows.
- Use single mouse clicks to access information and provide a consistent layout.
- Use a standard page design and the same symbols and icons throughout.
- Use the same set of navigation buttons in the same place on each page to move from one web page or section of the web site to another.

- Label each page in the same location with the name of the website.
- Incorporate text with the icon if possible, and use large buttons that do not require precise mouse movements for activation.
- Use pull down menus sparingly.
- Avoid automatically scrolling text. If manual scrolling is required, incorporate specific scrolling icons on each page.
- Incorporate buttons such as Previous Page and Next Page to allow the reader to review or move forward.
- Provide a site map to show how the site is organized.
- Use icons with text as hyperlinks.
- Offer a telephone number for those who would prefer to talk to a person or provide an e-mail address for questions or comments.
- Solicit unbiased comments from older adults through focus groups, usability testing or other means, to evaluate the accessibility and friendliness of the website (https://www.nlm.nih.gov/pubs/checklist).

Disability.gov

"Disability.gov is the federal government website for comprehensive information about disability-related programs, services, policies, laws and regulations. The site links to thousands of resources from many different federal government agencies, as well as state and local governments and nonprofit organizations across the country." (www.disability.gov)

Disability.gov is an "information and referral" website, which means that users will generally be referred to another website when seeking information from Disability.gov. For example, a resource about Social Security disability benefits will redirect a search to the Social Security Administration (www.ssa.gov). While Disability.gov cannot be responsible for the maintenance of information on these referred websites, new resources are added to Disability.gov's 10 main subject areas on a regular basis, including disability benefits, individual civil rights, education, employment, housing, and transportation. These resources can lead to a greater understanding of Social Security disability benefits, job accommodations for employees with disabilities, accessible housing, and organizations in your local area that can help people with disabilities find a job or live an independent life.

Disability.gov's "Guides to Information and Resources" provide information and links to other agencies, including state and local agencies about important topics like as follows:

- Assistive and Accessible Technologies
- Disability Benefits
- Disability Rights Laws
- Emergency Preparedness and Disaster Recovery
- Employment
- Family Caregivers
- Federal Government Grants
- Financial Help for Low-Income Individuals and Families
- Health Information and Resources
- Housing
- Self-Employment and Starting a Small Business
- Student Financial Aid
- Student Transition Planning
- Transportation

This comprehensive portal provides links to more than 14,000 resources from federal, state, and local government agencies; academic institutions; and nonprofit organizations. Consider putting a link to this and other government agencies on the library's website, under "E-government Resources."

Providing Accommodations

By making the effort to ensure that all of your library's services and programs are accessible to those with disabilities, you embrace an often overlooked library user group. In addition to the physical accessibility of your library, you should strive for an accessible website, which is, of course, a major source of access to your library's digital and physical collections, and a means of marketing programs and services. Be aware of the Americans with Disabilities Act requirements for facilities and provide these minimum accommodations:

- Have a Request for Accommodation policy and form in place and make it as simple and pleasant as possible (sample Request for Accommodation is in the Appendix F.
- Maintain an adequate number of accessible parking spaces and, when possible, police them.

- Maintain adequate openings, at least 32 inches wide, or automatic doors.
- Install handrails, ramps, and an elevator.
- Have accessible tables, computer tables, and desks available.

Remember, too, that large print key labels can assist patrons with low vision, there is software available to enlarge screen images, or use the zoom feature to enlarge. Have monitors of at least 17 inches in width and trackball mouse with good wrist rests. There are any number of other assistive technologies available for people with disabilities. Check with state assistive technology programs to learn more about the types of assistive technology available and any ways in which you might partner with agencies, or benefit from their services. A list of state assistive technology programs can be found at http://www.resnaprojects.org/allcontacts/statewidecontacts.html.

So much can be said about library services to people with disabilities. In many cases, people with disabilities are largely ignored, or merely tolerated, in libraries. It is our responsibility to ensure that people with disabilities have the same access to information and library services as everyone else in our communities.

MENTAL HEALTH ISSUES IN LIBRARIES

Library workers deal with people with mental health issues every day. For this reason, it is imperative to cultivate skills in dealing with people with these types of issues. Mental health issues vary greatly and are not always easily recognizable. It is not necessary that we are able to recognize issues for what they are, but that we are able to treat all of our library users with the sensitivity and patience that they deserve.

With the deinstitutionalization of the people with mental illness in the 1950s and 1960s, many people with these issues found themselves living on the streets. That number has only continued to grow as housing options began to and continue to diminish over time (National Coalition for the Homeless, 2005). It is no wonder that libraries, as public facilities dedicated to serving their communities, have become a haven for the homeless, often bringing mental health issues with them into the library.

Most often a person with mental illness might only need some special assistance or become an annoyance to other library users. Some of them might require some "mental health first aid." The National Council for Mental Health offers a course called "Mental Health First Aid"

(MHFA), with the intention of making mental health first aid as prevalent as cardiopulmonary resuscitation (CPR) instruction. According to the MHFA website, "Mental Health First Aid is an 8-hour course that teaches you how to identify, understand and respond to signs of mental illnesses and substance use disorders. The training gives you the skills you need to reach out and provide initial help and support to someone who may be developing and mental health or substance use problem or experiencing a crisis" (http://www.mentalhealthfirstaid.org/cs/about/). The MHFA website offers a tool for finding training in your area by zip code. In many areas, the course is free. In the Washington, DC, area, there are some courses offered for $25.00. Whether the course is free or offered at a nominal fee, this seems like a good investment for library staff.

For several years, the Missouri State Library partnered with the Missouri Department of Mental Health to provide library training in a number of areas related to library services to people with mental health issues in a project called Librarian411. I was honored to be part of that project. The results of this partnership included a number of videos demonstrating techniques for situations that may arise in public libraries, and while that particular project is no longer active, the videos created by Librarian411 can still be found on YouTube. Visit the Librarian411 web page with links to the YouTube videos at http://www.librarian411 .org. These videos cover a wide variety of topics including crisis preparation and response as well as a number of videos that deal with library services to people with physical disabilities and assistive technology in libraries. It is important that library workers have some skills in coping with emergency situations when they might arise, including emergencies involving mental illness. Safety is a main concern when working with the public, in any institution.

Have a Plan

Most libraries have disaster and emergency preparedness plans. Include plans for emergencies involving the homeless or people with mental illness. The Treatment Advocacy Center (TAC) of Arlington, Virginia, posts some very telling statistics on its website stating that a survey of 1,300 libraries reported that 9 out of 10 library workers have seen a person with mental illness disturb or affect other library users, 28 percent have seen a coworker assaulted by someone with mental illness, and 66 percent have had to change library policies and procedures to accommodate people with mental illness. In advocating for more assistance for people with mental illness, the TAC notes that "The problems facing libraries are part of the larger issue of the lack of available treatment for people with severe mental illness, especially for those who are discharged from mental hospitals without any follow up care. The result is an increase of people with mental illnesses who are homeless and turn to libraries and other public facilities because they just need somewhere to go" (http://www.treatmentadvocacycenter.org/home-page/71/1352).

In the article "Librarians Under Siege: How Can Librarians Protect Themselves Against Patrons Who Are Troubled or Violent?" Richard Bermack recounts a gun related incident at the Berkley Public Library (http://consumer.healthday.com/encyclopedia/work-and-health-41/occupational-health-news-507/librarians-under-siege-646477.html). Bermack shares advice from librarians who work with a diverse population every day and suggests taking conflict resolution and management courses and self-defense courses, having emergency procedures in place and understood and practiced by all staff, having a panic button, which calls police somewhere in the public service area, and professional evaluation of safety procedures.

"Safe Harbor: Policies and Procedures for a Safe Library," published by the Alliance Library System of Illinois and funded by a Library Services and Technology Act (LSTA) grant from the Illinois State Library, offers the following suggesting in the event of a violent confrontation in the library:

- "Any staff member who hears raised voices or sounds of a scuffle should investigate. Recruit other staff to quietly move other customers out of the way to a safer location.
- If you suspect violence is a possibility, call and alert other staff and administration. Use teamwork.
- Remain calm. Do not become angry and do not argue.
- Do not block exits.
- Do not invade their personal space. Maintain at least an arm's length away. This keeps staff out of punching or kicking range.
- If two adults are fighting, do not get between them.
- Call the police and describe the situation and location of the altercation. If they are not yet aware, call administration.
- Notice details so you can describe the combatants and the situation to authorities.
- Staff are expected to cooperate with the police and to serve as a witness in court if called upon to do so.

• Fill out an incident report and file it in the Director's Office. Administration may decide to ban the combatants from the library for a period of time."

The entire publication of "Safe Harbor" can be found on the Wyoming State Library website, as part of the *Wyoming Public Library Director's Handbook*.

MORE DETAILED PROGRAMMING IDEAS
Cultural Showcase

Offering immigrant populations the opportunity to showcase their culture not only benefits the group that you are showcasing but also offers the local community a chance to get to know their new neighbors. With immigrants increasingly under scrutiny in the United States, it is important that libraries assist them in all ways, including an opportunity to allow others to experience the food, music, art, and other customs of a culture. This program could be built around a number of different immigrant groups and provide a monthly program, possibly for several months, depending upon your location and demographics.

Learning goals:

• Get a glimpse into the culture of various immigrant populations
• Taste some of the foods from other cultures
• Learn about music, dance, or other art forms
• Allow for sharing and dissemination of information regarding immigrant cultures

Steps to take:

• Provide outreach to local immigrant populations by visiting churches, markets, or other locations where they gather. (Note that many members of immigrant populations are distrustful of government institutions.)
• Establish a relationship with members of the community and approach key members with the idea.
• Make the events long enough to highlight different aspects of a culture, preferably an afternoon or half-day event.
• Advertise via usual social and other media outlets, but try to get some local news coverage as well.

- Approach this project with the idea that you are not only building community relations, but also connecting with new library users.

Suggested reading for each event:

- Travel guides to the featured country of origin
- Histories and biographies of famous individuals from each country
- Fiction and poetry
- Children's books for families

By making these events family friendly and getting in some good marketing for them, cultural showcases might end up being a local favorite!

Alternative Book Group

In addition to regular book groups that might get together to talk over the latest best seller or biography, make members of the LGBT community feel welcome in the library. Like immigrants, LGBT people, and particularly the transgender, are coming under greater scrutiny and perhaps feeling more marginalized than in recent years. Having a book discussion club focusing on LGBT fiction or nonfiction about issues that they are facing would be a step toward making them feel more "at home" in the library.

Learning goals:

- Discover new works of fiction
- Learn about issues facing the LGBT community
- Participate in discussion of the issues in a welcoming and safe environment
- Learn more about library resources available to this community

Steps to take:

- Since each segment of this population will have different interests, perhaps focus on one group at a time
- Give each group a name other than "Alternative Book Group"
- Advertise on library social media and gauge interest
- Take suggestions for book titles for discussion
- Get one group established before starting another

Suggested authors/topics:

There are so many authors to choose from when forming an LGBT book discussion group, and group members will obviously have favorites that they want to share and discuss. Choose better known authors in the beginning, to get the ball rolling, and then allow the group or groups to set their own course. Here are a few authors to consider:

- Leslie Feinberg
- Cleve Jones
- Lillian Federman
- Sarah Waters
- Jeffrey Eugenides
- Rita Mae Brown
- Oscar Wilde
- Michael Chabon
- Jeannette Winterson

Giving the LGBT community a place to meet and hold book discussions, discussions on current events, speed dating, or any other type of programming based on gender or sexual preference falls under the library's scope of serving an entire community.

CONCLUSION

As difficult as the task may seem, treat all people, regardless of race, country of origin, physical or mental characteristics, gender, or sexual preference, by putting people first as the cornerstone of good customer service in libraries. The types of issues facing library workers today will not be resolved overnight, nor will they go away. Library workers can best equip themselves to deal with each situation, as it is, through training, effective policies and procedures, and the understanding that whether we like it or not, we are a "helping" profession. By reaching out to immigrant populations, people with disabilities, and having patience and policies in place when dealing with our library patrons, no matter what their life's circumstance may be, we can ensure continued and comprehensive library service in our local communities, now and in the future.

CHAPTER 10

Conclusion

TAKING ON LIFE'S CHALLENGES

The journey into adult maturity can be a long one, more so for some than others, and once our formal education ends, there can be little time left for the continued learning process. Libraries can play a key role in allowing adults to continue to learn and grow throughout their lifetime. As we all know, but sometimes fail to admit to ourselves, there is so much to learn in adulthood: How do I buy a home? How do I raise my child? How can I find a better job? What should I do to prepare for retirement? While pieces and parts of answers to all these question can be found with a "Google search," libraries offer the unique opportunity for people to find in-depth reading about all sorts of issues as well as assistance with finding reliable online resources, local community services, and eye-opening perspectives. Thoughtful and strategically planned programming can also assist adults of all ages with many of life's challenges.

Because we human beings spend the majority of our lifetimes as adults, the opportunities for libraries to provide successful programs and services to the grownups are many. It is up to each individual library to determine the types of programs that will be successful within each community or neighborhood and then plan accordingly. Grouping adults into categories of potential interest based on the predominant life changes that most of us experience as we grow older affords the chance to "get it right the first time" when it comes to planning for adult services. Being aware of changes in demographics through research and surveys can also contribute to being on target with library programs and services.

As young adults begin preparation for college or the workplace, settling down with a family, or pursuing career goals that leave little time for socializing, our libraries can become a destination for assistance with more serious matters like career and finance, or just a place to hang out with friends and enjoy games nights or book discussions. The online resources that libraries make available, at no cost, can also make a great impact in the lives of young working professionals.

As library users continue on their life's journey, it is important to keep them apprised and knowledgeable about what the library has to offer as well as offering programs and services that remain interesting, useful, and fresh throughout the lifespan. Looking closely at the later stages in life will benefit not only the library user but the library as well, as older adults turn into wonderful volunteers and supporters of the library.

SERVING THE ENTIRE COMMUNITY

Immigrant populations often come to the United States without an understanding of free library services, and it is important for libraries to ensure that each immigrant group is aware of the services offered and made available to as many as possible through outreach, coordinating with local organizations and social groups, translating library information into predominant foreign languages, and making every library user feel welcome and appreciated.

While the adults of all ages who we come in contact with on a daily basis come in all shapes and sizes, with varying information needs, physical and mental capabilities, levels of education, and different interests and backgrounds, it is important to remember that we are all people first and deserve the best that the library has to offer in the way of assistance, programming, and services.

While planning for adult services through the broad lens, I have suggested here would not necessarily catch every adult in the community in your library's web of activities and programs, it does give you a very simple "jumping off point," allowing you to add your own knowledge of local demographics, community and user needs, and regional tastes and interests to make your library services to adults the best they can be. We are adults much longer than we are children in life, and while it pays off in spades to give the kids all the benefits of story time and literacy programs, do not forget that we continue to grow and develop mentally throughout our lives. Here is hoping that your efforts to promote and ensure lifelong learning in your community are fruitful and that your local library reaps all of the benefits of community support and recognition that could come your way!

APPENDIX A

Customer Satisfaction Surveys

Courtesy of Library Research Service, Colorado State Library

Please take a moment to answer this anonymous survey about the library. All questions are optional.

Section 1: Please check <u>one</u> answer for each of the following:

1. How would you rate each of the following library services?

	Excellent	Good	Fair	Poor	Don't know/Not applicable
Customer service	☐	☐	☐	☐	☐
Collection (books, DVDs, music, newspapers, etc.)	☐	☐	☐	☐	☐
Programs (classes, storytimes, etc.)	☐	☐	☐	☐	☐
Online services (website, catalog, research databases, etc.)	☐	☐	☐	☐	☐
ILL (Interlibrary loan)	☐	☐	☐	☐	☐
Library policies	☐	☐	☐	☐	☐
Computers and printers	☐	☐	☐	☐	☐
Internet access	☐	☐	☐	☐	☐
Facilities	☐	☐	☐	☐	☐
Hours of operation	☐	☐	☐	☐	☐
Overall, how would you rate the library?	☐	☐	☐	☐	☐

Section 2: We value your opinions. Please answer the following questions:

2. What do you value *most* about the library?

3. How could the library or its services be improved, if at all?

Sample Medium Length Survey

Courtesy of Library Research Service, Colorado State Library

Please take a moment to answer this anonymous survey about the library. All questions are optional.

Section 1: Please check <u>one</u> answer for each of the following:

1. Do you have a library card?

	Yes	No
	☐	☐

2. On average, how often do you visit the library?

Daily	Weekly	Monthly	Less than once a month	Never
☐	☐	☐	☐	☐

3. How would you rate each of the following library services?

	Excellent	Good	Fair	Poor	Don't know/Not applicable
Customer service	☐	☐	☐	☐	☐
Collection (books, DVDs, music, newspapers, etc.)	☐	☐	☐	☐	☐
Programs (classes, storytimes, etc.)	☐	☐	☐	☐	☐
Online services (website, catalog, research databases, etc.)	☐	☐	☐	☐	☐
ILL (Interlibrary loan)	☐	☐	☐	☐	☐
Library policies	☐	☐	☐	☐	☐
Computers and printers	☐	☐	☐	☐	☐
Internet access	☐	☐	☐	☐	☐
Facilities	☐	☐	☐	☐	☐
Hours of operation	☐	☐	☐	☐	☐
Overall, how would you rate the library?	☐	☐	☐	☐	☐

4. How important is each of the following library services to you?

	Very Important	Important	Somewhat Important	Not Important	Don't know/Not Applicable
Borrowing materials (books, DVDs, music, etc.)	☐	☐	☐	☐	☐
Reference (research assistance from librarians)	☐	☐	☐	☐	☐
Programs (classes, storytimes, etc.)	☐	☐	☐	☐	☐
Computers and printers	☐	☐	☐	☐	☐
Help using computers, printers, etc.	☐	☐	☐	☐	☐
Study rooms/reading areas	☐	☐	☐	☐	☐
Community meeting rooms	☐	☐	☐	☐	☐
Internet access	☐	☐	☐	☐	☐
ILL (Interlibrary loan)	☐	☐	☐	☐	☐
Online services (website, catalog, research databases, etc.)	☐	☐	☐	☐	☐
Photocopier	☐	☐	☐	☐	☐
Newspapers and magazines	☐	☐	☐	☐	☐
Bookmobile	☐	☐	☐	☐	☐
Homebound services	☐	☐	☐	☐	☐
Overall, how important is the library to you and your family?	☐	☐	☐	☐	☐

Section 2: We value your opinions. Please answer the following questions:

5. What do you value *most* about the library?

6. How could the library or its services be improved, if at all?

7. How does the library benefit you or the community?

Thank you for your time! If you have questions about this survey or about the library, please contact us at yourcontactinfo@yourlibrary.com.

Sample Long Survey

Courtesy of Library Research Service, Colorado State Library

Please take a moment to answer this anonymous survey about the library. All questions are optional.

Section 1: Please check <u>one</u> answer for each of the following:

1. Do you have a library card?

	Yes	No
	☐	☐

2. On average, how often do you visit the library?

Daily	Weekly	Monthly	Less than once a month	Never
☐	☐	☐	☐	☐

3. How would you rate each of the following library services?

	Excellent	Good	Fair	Poor	Don't know/Not applicable
Customer service	☐	☐	☐	☐	☐
Collection (books, DVDs, music, newspapers, etc.)	☐	☐	☐	☐	☐
Programs (classes, storytimes, etc.)	☐	☐	☐	☐	☐
Online services (website, catalog, research databases, etc.)	☐	☐	☐	☐	☐
ILL (Interlibrary loan)	☐	☐	☐	☐	☐
Library policies	☐	☐	☐	☐	☐
Computers and printers	☐	☐	☐	☐	☐
Internet access	☐	☐	☐	☐	☐
Facilities	☐	☐	☐	☐	☐
Hours of operation	☐	☐	☐	☐	☐
Overall, how would you rate the library?	☐	☐	☐	☐	☐

4. How important is each of the following library services to you?

	Very Important	Important	Somewhat Important	Not Important	Don't know/Not Applicable
Borrowing materials (books, DVDs, music, etc.)	☐	☐	☐	☐	☐
Reference (research assistance from librarians)	☐	☐	☐	☐	☐
Programs (classes, storytimes, etc.)	☐	☐	☐	☐	☐
Computers and printers	☐	☐	☐	☐	☐
Help using computers, printers, etc.	☐	☐	☐	☐	☐
Study rooms/reading areas	☐	☐	☐	☐	☐
Community meeting rooms	☐	☐	☐	☐	☐
Internet access	☐	☐	☐	☐	☐
ILL (Interlibrary loan)	☐	☐	☐	☐	☐
Online services (website, catalog, research databases, etc.)	☐	☐	☐	☐	☐
Photocopier	☐	☐	☐	☐	☐
Newspapers and magazines	☐	☐	☐	☐	☐
Bookmobile	☐	☐	☐	☐	☐
Homebound services	☐	☐	☐	☐	☐
Overall, how important is the library to you and your family?	☐	☐	☐	☐	☐

5. How do you typically find out about library programs? Check all that apply.
   ☐ Library website
   ☐ Social media (Facebook or Twitter)
   ☐ Newspaper
   ☐ Library newsletter
   ☐ Signs or flyers in the library
   ☐ Word of mouth
   ☐ Library staff
   ☐ Don't know/Not applicable
   ☐ Other—please specify: _____

Section 2: We value your opinions. Please answer the following questions:

6. What do you value *most* about the library?

7. How could the library or its services be improved, if at all?

8. How does the library benefit you or the community?

Section 3: Please tell us about yourself so that we may better serve you. Please check one answer for each of the following.

9. How old are you?
   ☐ 12 or under
   ☐ 13–18
   ☐ 19–24
   ☐ 25–64
   ☐ 65 or older

10. What gender best describes you?
    ☐ Male
    ☐ Female

11. What is the highest level of education you have completed?
    ☐ Some high school
    ☐ High school graduate or GED
    ☐ Some college
    ☐ College degree or higher

12. What is your preferred language?
    ☐ English
    ☐ Spanish
    ☐ Vietnamese
    ☐ Other—please specify: _____

13. What is your employment status?
    ☐ Employed or self-employed
    ☐ Homemaker
    ☐ Retired
    ☐ Unemployed

Thank you for your time! If you have questions about this survey or about the library, please contact us at yourcontactinfo@yourlibrary.com.

APPENDIX B

Competency Index for the Library Field, Adult Services

Compiled by WebJunction
Updated February 2014

Public Services Competencies
All of the services that interface directly with the library's users come together under the heading of public services. These frontline staff anticipate and meet the needs of users in the most visible way. Fully supported by all of the other sectors and departments, they work to provide the best possible programs and services to the library community.

Adult and Older Adult Services
Libraries have the capacity to inspire, engage, and support community members of all ages. Libraries provide an array of opportunities for adult patrons from diverse backgrounds.

Outreach
Designs and implements library services to engage and meet the needs of the community

- Uses a variety of ongoing methods to determine the interests of adults in the community (obtains demographic data, surveys users and nonusers, follows current events, collects input from frontline staff, etc.)
- Analyzes demographic and other data collected about the community and develops a wide variety of services to meet the needs and interests of target audiences
- Identifies potential partner organizations within the institution or in the community that have compatible goals and objectives to serve

adults, and develops cooperative services and programs to extend and enhance library service

- Aligns all services and programs with library policies and procedures
- Evaluates all services, using appropriate evaluation strategies (evaluation forms, customer satisfaction surveys, input from frontline staff and other stakeholders, etc.), and uses the results to improve future services

Defines and implements outreach services for the library community to increase use of library services and to reach underserved populations

- Identifies individuals and groups not adequately served (those with disabilities, homebound, institutionalized, remote, non-English speaking, immigrant, low literacy, etc.)
- Determines the particular needs of each target audience and designs a variety of programs and services appropriate to them
- Identifies individuals and groups not currently served by the library, determines needs, develops programs and services, and promotes them to the nonusers with targeted marketing
- Aligns all outreach efforts with the library's overall goals and objectives
- Determines the best means to deliver library services to remote users (mail, bookmobile, online, multimedia) appropriate to library resources
- Designs programs and builds collections and information resources to meet the special language and literacy needs of the community
- Collaborates with other community groups to meet the literacy needs of target audiences

Uses online tools and communities to engage with and provide services to users

- Understands and articulates the importance of engaging with users virtually
- Investigates and evaluates tools for virtual engagement, and identifies those most applicable to the library's services and community needs
- Determines objectives for enhancing library services and access, and acquires proficiency with selected tools to provide effective library services
- Uses social networking to interact with users and meet their information needs

- Understands established policies and procedures for online engagement with users
- Devises strategies to keep up with emerging tools and techniques, and connects with professional communities to seek and share best practices

Adult (General) Programming
Designs, implements, and sponsors library programs that provide opportunities for information, entertainment, and lifelong learning

- Demonstrates ability to be creative, promote new ideas and identify a variety of tools and techniques to create interesting and engaging programs
- Aligns programs with the library's goals and objectives and with the identified interests and needs of the community
- Provides resources and programming that serve the needs of makers and do-it-yourselfers in the community
- Actively involves users in planning, implementing, and evaluating programs
- Creates programs that encourage audience participation and dialogue and encourage peer-to-peer knowledge sharing
- Promotes the library's programs to the community in coordination with marketing efforts
- Develops programs to acknowledge and celebrate the cultural diversity of the community
- Develops programs that encourage learning and dialogue in support of twenty-first-century themes, such as civic literacy, health literacy, environmental literacy, financial literacy, and global awareness
- Understands the value of games and gaming for adults, and develops gaming programs
- Identifies program venues outside of the library
- Coordinates with collection development efforts in support of programming
- Evaluates programs using appropriate evaluation strategies (evaluation forms, debrief with presenters, input from frontline staff, etc.), and uses results to improve future programming efforts

Older Adult Services and Programming
Research has shown that older adults (defined broadly as patrons aged 55+) wish to remain engaged in the community and to continue learning. Libraries can help them achieve both of these goals.

Designs and implements library services to meet the needs and interests of older adults in the community

- Analyzes demographic and other data collected about older adults in the community to assess their unique needs
- Develops a wide variety of services to meet the needs and interests of older adults and of their families and caregivers, as members of the Sandwich Generation
- Understands the range of older adults (baby boomers to the elderly) and identifies their particular needs and interests, acknowledging the range of skills, knowledge, strengths, and limitations they bring to the library
- Recognizes that older adults need twenty-first-century skills and provides opportunities for building the five literacies (e.g., basic, information, civic and social, health, and financial)
- Creates programs and other opportunities for learning and interaction, including intergenerational activities and opportunities for civic participation
- Partners with organizations within the institution or in the community that have compatible goals and objectives to serve older adults, and develops cooperative services and programs to extend and enhance older adult services
- Identifies and maintains regular communication with agencies, institutions, and organizations serving older adults in the community
- Engages older adults for input when planning, implementing, and evaluating programs and services

Defines and implements outreach services to increase older adults' use of library services and to reach underserved populations

- Ensures that older adult audiences are included in the target audiences for the library's outreach efforts
- Identifies older adults who are unable to visit the library, determines their special needs for library resources, and determines the best means to deliver library services to them
- Understands and addresses specialized concerns of some older adult users (disliking change, loss of personal freedoms or controls, slowly adopting new technologies, etc.)
- Designs, implements, and sponsors library programs for older adults that provide information, entertainment, and opportunities for lifelong learning

- Acknowledges the knowledge and experience of older adults, and provides opportunities for them to use these lifetime strengths in volunteering with the library
- Creates programs that provide older adults with an opportunity to interact and share their knowledge, experiences, and stories
- Actively involves older adults in planning, implementing, and evaluating programs
- Promotes the library's programs to the older adult community in coordination with marketing efforts
- Recognizes the challenges and opportunities that digital literacy provides for older adults, and provides learning assistance to foster confidence and learning
- Understands the potential of games and other group and individual activities to foster cognitive and mental stimulation and social involvement, and identifies a variety of methods to meet those needs

Readers' Advisory
Assists users with choosing popular and recreational reading, viewing, and listening choices

- Demonstrates a broad knowledge of the library's collection and of a wide range of materials of interest to library readers
- Demonstrates the ability to read widely, formulate connections between resources and converse with users about the resources
- Understands the theory of appeal, listens carefully to information elicited from the user, and bases recommendations on an interpretation of what appeals to the user
- Communicates succinctly but effectively the character and appeal of a book, both in writing and speaking
- Identifies and recommends a selection of materials that align with what appeals to the user
- Seeks feedback from readers on recommended materials, and adjusts future recommendations accordingly
- Creates booklists, read-alikes, read-arounds, book-talks, displays, electronic documents, and other special tools to increase access to library resources and promote their use
- Engages with users virtually as well as face to face for readers' advisory interactions
- Uses social networking sites and tools to spark conversations with community members about titles, authors, and reading

- Implements reader input forms (both print and online) to provide personalized service to readers
- Explores and implements ways technology can connect readers' advisory to the library's catalog, such as reading lists

Develops strategies and sources to stay well informed as a readers' advisor

- Identifies and uses a variety of readers' advisory resources to identify materials
- Maintains an ongoing knowledge of major new authors, fiction genres, nonfiction subjects, and current releases
- Keeps current with popular culture through a variety of channels
- Connects with professional communities to seek and share best practices for readers' advisory

Reference
Develops and maintains a collection of reference resources to meet community needs

- Discovers and assesses needs of the community and identifies how the library can help
- Demonstrates knowledge of the reference collection, including both print and online resources
- Provides a variety of readily accessible reference resources that meet identified community needs, such as job seeking and health information seeking
- Prepares bibliographies, subject collections, and other user guides to resources in a variety of formats, and creates tutorials to help users navigate information sources
- Ensures that information sources are available in formats accessible virtually, including users who are accessing via a mobile device
- Compiles and maintains information about community resources appropriate to users' needs, and connects users with these resources when appropriate
- Performs ongoing evaluation of the currency and usefulness of the reference collection, and makes recommendations for acquisition or deselection
- Facilitates library users' requests for information
- Maintains a friendly and approachable demeanor that invites interaction

- Establishes rapport with information seekers quickly
- Communicates effectively in both face-to-face and online interactions
- Practices effective reference interviewing skills to identify and satisfy a user's needs
- Addresses the information-seeking behaviors and needs of users without bias across the spectrum of age, race, gender, ethnicity, ability, or economic status
- Serves as a guide for collaborative and participatory learning
- Provides support for users and their self-directed learning endeavors
- Provides instruction and support to users that enhances critical thinking and problem-solving abilities
- Uses current technology tools for research, and makes exploration of new tools and platforms an ongoing effort
- Acknowledges users' knowledge, and engages them as partners in seeking information and choosing resources
- Answers questions knowledgeably, providing information of an appropriate scope and reading level
- Personalizes and customizes resources for the particular needs and priorities of individuals
- Evaluates the success of reference services through feedback from staff, users, and other stakeholders
- Identifies opportunities for instruction, and empowers users to improve their own information-seeking ability

Demonstrates ability to meet information-seeking needs of users

- Demonstrates flexibility and adapts to the changing ways in which users interact with information
- Demonstrates advanced search skills
- Understands and performs effective search queries, using multiple resources and search strategies
- Synthesizes information from a variety of resources, and evaluates results for quality and accuracy
- Demonstrates proficiency in website editing in order to update online resources and utilize various technologies to interact most effectively with online users

APPENDIX C

Adult Volunteer Application

T*hank you for your interest in volunteering at the San Juan Island Library. We look forward to talking with you about your application.*

Volunteer's Contact Information

	Date:
Name	
Mailing Address	
City ST Zip Code	
Daytime Phone Number	
Alternate Phone Number	
Email Address	

Availability

How many HOURS PER WEEK do you wish to volunteer? _____

Are you volunteering to fulfill a community service requirement?

    If so, is there a TOTAL NUMBER of hours you need to volunteer?

        YES NO Total hours needed: _____

    Is there a DEADLINE by which those hours need to be completed?

        YES NO Deadline: _____

Place an X for the times you are available to volunteer. Circle the Xs for your preferred hours.

	Sundays	Mondays	Tuesdays	Wednesdays	Thursdays	Fridays	Saturdays
9-10am	closed						
10-Noon	closed						
Noon-1pm							
1-3pm							
3-5pm							
5-6pm	closed						closed
6-8pm	closed	closed		closed		closed	closed

Are you willing to be "on call" for tasks as they arise?   YES   NO

Interests

___ Check-in, shelving & shelf reading
___ Morning prep for library opening
___ Helping with TEND-A-SHELF
___ Helping with ENGLISH CLASS
___ Helping with LIVE & LEARN (Adult Programs)

___ Helping with outreach & book delivery
___ Processing new books & materials
___ Mending books & materials
___ Special projects
___ Other: _____

Skills or Talents You Would Like to Share

Person to Notify in Case of Emergency

Name & Relationship	
City ST Zip Code	
Mailing Address	
Primary Phone Number	
Alternate Phone Number	
Email Address	

Agreement & Signature

I understand that the San Juan Island Library reserves the right to screen volunteers and accept or reject any applications, and to place volunteers in specific locations & positions based on the needs of the Library.

Signature

Date

Revised: 2013.August.27 LO
File location: Plaza / Volunteers / SJLIB Volunteer Application - Adult
Distribution: Reference desk file drawer

(Reprinted courtesy of San Juan Island Library)

Volunteer Policy

I. Purpose

The following policy is designed to promote a maximum degree of excellence in the library's volunteer program. The North Liberty Community Library's volunteers are an important extension of the Library's staff. Volunteers perform a wide variety of tasks that are vital to the institution.

II. Definition of a Volunteer

One who performs a service of his or her own free will; one who contributes time, energy, and talents directly or on behalf of the North Liberty Community Library and is not paid by Library funds.

III. Utilization of Volunteers

In order to achieve the vision and mission statement of the North Liberty Community Library, we view the active participation of citizens, of a variety of ages, as a valuable resource to the Library. After fulfilling Library procedures, the Library accepts and encourages the involvement of volunteers at most levels of the Library and within appropriate programs and activities. Volunteers shall be extended the right to be given meaningful assignments, the right to be treated as an equal, the right to effective supervision, the right to full involvement and participation, and the right to recognition of good work.

IV. Guidelines for Volunteers

1. Each volunteer is required to complete a volunteer application and to wear a volunteer badge while performing volunteer work.

Volunteers must be approved by Library staff prior to performance of assigned tasks.

2. Volunteers will receive regular training from designated library staff.
3. Volunteers may start service in 6th grade with parental permission.
4. Special accommodations will be made upon request.
5. A background check may be made on each adult volunteer.
6. Volunteers will show respect to patrons, other volunteers and staff.
7. Discriminatory or racist incidents will not be tolerated.
8. Procedures and requirements for the volunteer will vary with age of volunteer.
9. Should a volunteer have a grievance with a staff person, another volunteer or library patron, every attempt will be made to resolve the situation with library administration.
10. The North Liberty Community Library reserves the right to terminate the services of the volunteer, if merited.
11. Volunteers may be used to increase current Library services.
12. Volunteers may not be used to establish and maintain new library services.
13. Volunteers will not be used to replace or reduce the number of paid staff.
14. Volunteers will be covered with respect to liability insurance in relation to their duties at the library.
15. Volunteers are recognized as contributors to the goals and services of the Library.
16. Volunteers are responsible for maintaining the confidentiality of all library information. Failure to maintain confidentiality will result in immediate termination.
17. The Library staff will, upon request, provide letters of reference for a volunteer, if deemed appropriate.
18. All personal information about the volunteer is for internal use only.
19. Volunteers are prohibited from being under the influence of using, possessing, selling, or otherwise being involved with illegal substances and alcohol while volunteering.

Reviewed/Approved by the Library Board of Trustees, May 2016

(Courtesy of North Liberty Community Library, North Liberty, Iowa)

APPENDIX E

Library-by-Mail Homebound Application Form

Contact Information

Full Legal Name: * _____

First, Middle, Last

Street Address: * _____

City: * _____

State: * _____

Zip Code: * _____

* You must live within the Mid-Continent Public Library service area to qualify for this service

Phone Number: * _____

Best time of day to receive phone calls:

○ Morning
○ Afternoon

Email Address:

Reading Interest

Select all that apply:

Fiction Interests:

☐ Bestsellers

☐ Christian Fiction

☐ Espionage/Military

☐ Fantasy

☐ Historical Fiction

☐ Horror

☐ Mystery

☐ Paranormal

☐ Romance

☐ Science Fiction

☐ Thrillers

☐ Westerns/Gunfighter

Nonfiction Interests:

☐ Animals

☐ Biography

☐ History

☐ Military

☐ Religion

☐ Science

☐ Self-Help

☐ True Crime

Favorite Authors:

```

```

You can enter several author names separated by commas.

Type of books needed:

☐ Large Print

☐ Regular Print

☐ Paperback

Type of audiovisual needed:

☐ Audiobooks

☐ Music CD

☐ DVD

☐ Blue-ray

I do not want materials that contain:

☐ Strong Language

☐ Sex

☐ Violence

Would you like us to select materials for you based on your interests?: *

○ Do not select materials for me. Send only the titles I request.

○ Please select materials for me. I may also request specific titles whenever I wish.

Comments:

```
┌─────────────────────────────────────────┐
│                                         │
│                                         │
│                                         │
│                                         │
│                                         │
└─────────────────────────────────────────┘
```

Do you have any additional comments or instructions?

Certification allows the library to ship materials to qualified customers without being charged postage.

Authorization*

I declare that I am homebound and unable to go to the Mid-Continent Public Library due to health, mobility, advanced age, visual impairment, blindness, physical disability, permanent, or temporary incapacity.

☐ I am Homebound

Leave this field blank:_____

Submit My Application

APPENDIX F

Reasonable Accommodation Request Form

The Allegany County Library System provides reasonable accommodations, by request, for physical access, communications, or other needs to ensure services, activities, and programs are available to people with disabilities. For the purpose of this form, accommodation requests will be considered for persons who have disabilities that are expected to last at least six months.

Name: _____ Date:_____
Address: _____
City: _____ State: _____ Zip Code: _____
Phone: _____ (Alt. Phone): _____
Library branch(s) most often visited (circle all that apply) Frostburg George's Creek
LaVale South Cumberland Washington Street Westernport
Email (optional): _____
Library card number (optional): _____
I am requesting the following accommodation(s): (check all that apply)
Circulation Access: Check here if you have a condition that makes it difficult or impossible to check out library materials. Please describe the accommodation you are requesting:

_____

_____

Program/Services Access: Check here if you are unable to participate in a library program or service due to a disability and describe the accommodation you are requesting below.

_____

_____

Other: Describe the accommodation you are requesting and how it will assist you in your use of Library programs or services: (Attach additional sheets as necessary.)

_____

_____

_____

_____

Please submit your completed form to:
Allegany County Library System
31 Washington Street
Cumberland, MD, 21502
Your request will be addressed as quickly as possible. Please note that certification by a Health Care Provider may be required.

This form is for library use only. All information will be kept confidential.

Index

About the Author

ANN ROBERTS is a reference librarian at the U.S. Patent and Trademark Office, Public Search Facility. She has worked in public, academic, and government libraries as well as with historical collections. She is author or coauthor of three books in the Crash Course series by Libraries Unlimited: *Crash Course in Library Gift Programs: The Reluctant Curator's Guide to Caring for Archives, Books, and Artifacts in a Library Setting*; *Crash Course in Library Services for Seniors* (with Stephanie G. Bauman); and *Crash Course in Library Services to People with Disabilities* (with Richard J. Smith).